Ride or Die

Ride or Die

Loving Through Tragedy,
A Husband's Memoir

Jarie Bolander

Published by SparkPress, a BookSparks imprint,
A division of SparkPoint Studio, LLC
Phoenix, Arizona, USA, 85007
www.gosparkpress.com

Published 2023
Printed in the United States of America
Print ISBN: 978-1-68463-210-7
E-ISBN: 978-1-68463-211-4
Library of Congress Control Number: 2023902857

Interior Design by Tabitha Lahr

To Jane,

*for teaching me the true meaning
of love and commitment. You will always
have a place in my heart.*

Author's Note

Grief and loss are so personal, and yet we all have shared experiences that warrant an attempt at understanding them. I make sense of the world after loss by writing, and this memoir is my attempt to understand and process a time in my life that was filled with joy, love, sorrow, grief, and loss.

There are countless books about marriage, relationships, trauma, struggles, grief, love, and loss. I recommend *A Grief Observed*, by C. S. Lewis; *The Year of Magical Thinking*, by Joan Didion; *Option B*, by Sheryl Sandberg and Adam Grant; *Tell Me More*, by Kelly Corrigan; *Grace and Grit*, by Ken Wilber; and *This Is How*, by Augusten Burroughs. Each of these helped me make sense of the random and chaotic nature of life and to craft the words that ended up in this memoir.

I've relied on memories of events I experienced when I was dealing with an awful lot of pain, stress, grief, and anxiety, but I've done my level best to describe the situations, dialogue, and other details as accurately as possible. I went back to my journals, emails from Jane, and the many text messages I saved. Even with all those in-the-moment sources, I'm sure I got some of it wrong, and there will be those who remember things differently.

One of the ways I tried to keep true to Jane's and my experience was to include lightly edited Care Circle emails. These emails are the ones that Jane and I wrote to our extended family and friends to share the journey we were on. In addition to the emails, I include text exchanges between Jane and me. These are the actual words we shared. I did this to be true to the experience, and so that the reader could get a glimpse of who Jane was and how we interacted.

Coming to terms with my own trauma and grief journey, and helping others get through theirs, were central to my thinking about what I wanted this book to be. But as I got ready to put the finished story into the world, I came back to the first and most important reason for telling this story: I wanted to give my readers a glimpse of my beloved Jane—the love, anxiety, compassion, anger, frustration, humor, and courage she showed as she navigated her life from start to finish. For me, this puts into context what the wedding vows we took meant to us. So often the words we say are only that—until we put them into practice.

Preface

I never gave my marriage vows much thought until I had to put them into practice.

To have and to hold from this day forward, for better, for worse, for richer, for poorer, in sickness and in health, to love, cherish, and to obey, till death do us part.

In sickness and in health . . . till death do us part. That's the part I didn't imagine I'd grow to have a new appreciation for.

The origins of the wedding vows come from the Book of Common Prayer by Thomas Cranmer, archbishop of Canterbury, first published in 1549 and only slightly modified in 1662. The 1662 change was minor, swapping the original *"till death us do part"* to *"till death do us part."*

My first wife, Margaret, and I said those vows at San Francisco City Hall, under the rotunda with the late morning sun streaming in, with whichever marriage commissioner was available for our prepaid appointment on August 25, 2002.

Till death do us part.

That's the couple's prompt to say, "I do," and once each person has said those words, that's the commissioner's prompt to announce the couple as husband and wife. Much rejoicing. Kissing and clapping.

My only recollection of the importance of a vow, other than my forced Methodist upbringing, came from Michael O'Flynn, professor of electrical engineering at San Jose State University, where I learned, among other things, the odds of betting on the ponies and the dire consequences of breaking our vow to him to show up to every class ready and willing to learn.

Professor O'Flynn loved betting on the ponies. Every test or quiz in his Probabilities, Random Variables, and Random Processes class (named after his book by the same name) had at least one, if not two, questions about the odds of betting on horse race parlays. Up until then, my only experience with horse racing was the "dollar dogs and beers" at Bay Meadows, where my high school friends and I would spend the better part of a Wednesday evening "winning a twenty," which had little to do with horse racing and everything to do with not getting sick in the port-o-john after spending said twenty on "dogs and beers," with more emphasis on the beers. His other favorite was drawing balls from an urn. I always loved how O'Flynn would say "urn" in his drawn-out thick Irish brogue.

He would show up to class with wispy, windblown white hair, chalk dust along the bulging midline of his belly from erasing the blackboard as he'd write up his next proof or example of how you could beat the track. It was 1993, and while the transition from chalk to dry-erase board was in full swing, O'Flynn's belly never got the memo, or didn't care to upgrade.

His class was a requirement that most of us hated. It was heavy on math even for an engineer, but it was the foundation of communications theory, which is all about signal, noise, and loss on transmission lines or media. Cable modems and Wi-Fi routers work because of the protocols that were developed to handle when a packet of information is lost.

The real world was "random and chaotic," he'd say. "Without understanding that, your lives will be full of pain and misery. I only wish I could drop water on your heads as you learn all this.

That way, you'd remember." He never did figure out how to drop water on our heads during class, but he did make us enforce our vow to come to his class ready to learn, and his vow to us in turn was that he would correct any test or quiz before our next class.

"By threat of death, I shall vow to grade these quizzes. Even if I have the steepest fever or I have to fall out of bed to crawl the half mile to this class." He never broke that vow and neither did I—at least not to him.

My failed marriage to Margaret was not random, but it was chaotic. It was the cumulation of a series of events both unfortunate and unavoidable. The chaos that sparked it all was the sudden diagnosis of stage 4 lung cancer of my mother-in-law, Margit.

The challenge one faces when dealing with the life-and-death circumstances of a loved one diagnosed with cancer is immense. How people handle it depends largely on whether or not it's their first rodeo. Even then, every illness is unique, yet the rhythms of the health-care system echo with the familiar "standard of care," "everyone is different," "we just don't know," and/or "you need to make a decision quickly on this."

In these initial moments of stress and strain, one tends to focus their available cortisol and adrenaline on the why. *Why did she get cancer? Why now? Why is this happening to me?* This is futile.

Instead, the focus should be on the *What do we need to do?* since no amount of understanding the *why* will reverse the fact that your loved one has cancer.

We only found out Margit had lung cancer in the first place because she complained that her ribs hurt after bouncing over one of those suburban DIY speed bumps that accompany the sign that says: DRIVE LIKE YOUR KIDS PLAY HERE. By the time she was diagnosed, the cancer had spread to her bones; that rib pain was being caused by tiny hairline fractures splintering her ribs like cracks in a dropped smartphone screen.

Cancer was the second-leading cause of death in the US. When Margit got her diagnosis, everyone wanted to know her chances. Cancer survival chances are reported in the "five-year survival rate." The rate is a percentage of those still alive five years after being diagnosed. Most doctors will tell you, "Everyone is different," or, "We'll do everything we can for her," or, "Don't focus on the numbers. Focus on the treatment." Wise advice.

The fact that the five-year survival rate for stage 4 lung cancer was 7 percent at best and 3 percent at worst solidified the focus on what needed to be done rather than why she got it.

Even the five-year survival rate had probabilities, since a lot depended on when people found out, other comorbidities, how they tolerated treatment, and who was treating them. I think that's why the world seems so random and chaotic when people find out. They have no frame of reference for what to expect other than some Hallmark made-for-TV movie pamphlets at worst, or prior experience at best. Sure, there are plenty of Internet searches that can bring up all sorts of experiences, statistics, and remedies, but being in it seems to short-circuit logic and reason all while trying to make some sense out of it all.

Margit died six months after her diagnosis.

The same search for cause, for the *Why did this happen?* can also apply to ending a marriage and finding love again. Again, we tend to focus on why something went wrong rather than what we need to do in order not to repeat the same mistakes.

Frames of reference. Why do things happen?

The world is random and chaotic.

CHAPTER 1

It's Probably Just the Flu

Jane and I had been married a little less than a year when we started on the baby train. A lot of Jane's friends were working on their second kid, so we felt pressure to perform even though we were starting late, having only met two years prior to getting married, and me being ten years older.

"Getting preggers," as Jane put it, turned out to be both easy and hard. Easy in that it happened on our first try, yet hard in that she had a miscarriage.

Fertility was a tricky topic for couples. The usual course of action was to look at the woman, especially if she'd had a miscarriage. The medical literature showed that if the man's sperm could knock her up, then there was a high chance—90-plus percent—that something was wrong with the woman. Those might be the facts, but on the baby train, one must do what one is asked. The engineer in me wanted to rely on the facts and data, but I knew that was not going to be enough. After all, I loved Jane, and Jane wanted a baby—and I wanted to be a supportive and nonjudgmental partner. So, I took vitamins, stopped drinking, wore boxers, ate clean, and cut back on coffee. It was actually a small price to pay to ease the stress and strain I knew she was under. I knew she would do the same for me.

After Jane's second miscarriage, the doctors did more blood tests, including several during the months leading up to the 2015 Christmas holidays, which still made us hopeful newlyweds after celebrating our first anniversary in late October.

Most of the results were normal, but some of the complete blood counts (CBCs) were too low—specifically, Jane's white blood cell counts were off. Nothing to worry about, they told us. Jane was Taiwanese American, and in some Asian populations, that happens. No one knows why. As they say—lies, damned lies, and statistics.

"Kaiser said I could get the blood work in Walnut Creek. Can we swing by before we go home?" Jane made this request as I was running back and forth to our car in the mid-morning chill, loading it to travel back home to San Francisco from her parents' house in Walnut Creek.

"Do we have to? We're always packing too much stuff in. I just want to get home," I said. I was tired and wanted to chill. We'd had three days of family and friends over Christmas, and we were heading home on the twenty-sixth—a day earlier than I had thought, which made me happy.

My enthusiasm for leaving had nothing to do with my feelings about Jane's family. We often spent weekends with them, and I enjoyed the dinner table banter, home cooking, and stories of Jane's childhood—especially when they would bring out the Taiwanese equivalent of Barbizon modeling pictures, complete with blown-out Farrah Fawcett hair, midriff-revealing shirts, and Vaseline lens to soften her features so she looked like she was plucked straight out of a wet dream.

My eagerness to get on the road stemmed from the fact that I was a highly functional introvert. Too many people exhausted me. We had even gone to premarital couples therapy to work through Jane's complaint, which amounted to: "Why doesn't Jarie talk to me?" My answer: I needed a break from people to recharge. But Jane didn't operate that way. People gave her more energy.

"It will take like five minutes," she persisted. "No one will be around. You can sit in the car. I want to get this done, and we're driving right past it. One less thing to do next week."

I didn't want to give in, but I so often did with her. Not because I felt guilty or wanted to please; I had plenty of experience with that in my past relationships. This was different since this was her health and not some random thing to check off her infinite to-do list.

"I just want to crash before we go to dinner. Do we really have to do it today?" I whined.

"You can get a coffee while I get it done. Pacific Bay is right across the street." She was smiling. She knew I loved their coffee. Well, coffee in general, about as much as whiskey.

I rolled my eyes and huffed. "All right. We can go."

Jane was already eager to get back on the baby train, but her periods were still heavier than usual, and the plan was to wait a couple more months, take all the vitamins, do more tests—the reason for our detour to the clinic that day—and look closely into her blood work.

I dropped her off around 11 a.m. By the time I'd parked at the coffee shop, not ten minutes later, she was already texting me to come get her.

As we sped home toward San Francisco, Jane texted one of her friends. She was always multitasking—talking to me, texting, or typing on her computer, even in the car.

"Ooh. I almost forgot," she turned to me and announced, "we got into the *Star Wars* premiere as well. Mike hooked us up!"

Jane had her own publicity firm, JSY PR & Marketing, and with professional athletes, start-ups, and nonprofits for clients, she always got invited to movie premieres, one of the best perks of her business. I was honestly looking forward to geeking out at the premiere. I'd seen the original a hundred times as a kid. Plus, I was trying to be more like Jane in her zest for life. She always found the time to do something fun every week. I, on the other hand, was not that good at having fun for the sake of fun—but I was learning.

Traffic was light, and we made the normally forty-five minutes door-to-door to our apartment in Pacific Heights in less than thirty-five minutes. As I huffed our suitcases up the stairs, Jane's phone buzzed, but she didn't recognize the number.

"Ignore it," I told her. "It's the day after Christmas *and* a Friday. Whoever it is can wait." I never answered my cell if I didn't recognize the number. Too many salespeople trying to sell me crappy insurance or "a great vacation time-share in Florida." So annoying.

"It might be the restaurant confirming. See, it's a 415 number." She showed me the number, then answered while I carried the suitcases to the bedroom.

"Hello. Hmm. Okay. Right now? Okay. Yeah, we live close." Jane followed me, perplexed, and hung up the phone. "That was Kaiser. They want me to come into the ER right now to do more tests."

"What? More tests. Now? Did they say why?" As I put our bags down, my stomach tightened more from annoyance than tension.

"No. They said they saw the results of the blood test from Walnut Creek this morning and need to do more. They said it can't wait till Monday." Jane looked annoyed. *That was fast*, I thought. Barely an hour between sample and results.

We had been called to the ER before, after the second miscarriage, for what seemed like no reason. Better to be safe than sorry, they had said.

"Well, let's get going then. Hopefully, we can get out fast, with plenty of time to get ready for dinner." I was thankful it wasn't New Year's Eve—that would be a shit show for sure.

THE DRIVE TO KAISER'S ER TOOK LESS than five minutes from our apartment. Check-in took less than a minute. The analog clock over the entrance to the ER indicated 12:17 p.m. as we were escorted in. They had been expecting us and swept Jane right into the middle holding pen with a dozen or so beds in a row separated by flimsy curtains that stuck along their tracks as you pulled them apart. The ER was so busy that they had patients on gurneys lined up in the hallway. We passed an old man with abrasions on his face and a chipped tooth from what looked like a fall. He was softly moaning for a nurse to help him. It was hardly private, but better than the germ-filled waiting room that had turned into a M.A.S.H. unit due to a nasty flu that was going around.

I sat on an uncomfortable orange plastic chair, holding Jane's hand as she tried to text her doctor friend Mary with the other, but the reception deep in the bowels of the ER was horrible. As usual, the smells and bells of the monitors made me anxious. The soft moans of the old man we passed on our way in were also not helping. But we only waited five minutes before two white-coated doctors, both female, struggled to push/pull the sticky curtain open to visit us.

"Mrs. Bolander, my name is Dr. Clayton, and this is Dr. Barber. We are in charge of your care here in the ER. Do you know why you're here?" said the older, gray-haired one, with dark circles under her eyes—the universal sign of being up all night.

"No. All they told me on the phone was that my blood test this morning was abnormal and I needed to come into the ER."

"Yes, Mrs. Bolander. That's correct. Your blood work is abnormal, and we also noticed the petechiae on your stomach. How long has that been going on?" Small patches of red dots, or petechiae, had been on her stomach and legs since the miscarriage. We were told that sometimes that happens because the severe cramping breaks the tiny blood vessels on the surface of the skin.

"I don't know. Maybe a couple of weeks. Why? What's wrong?"

Dr. Clayton paused and looked to Dr. Barber to pipe in. "We're not exactly sure yet. We need to talk with the oncologist who's on call to see what he has to say," Dr. Barber said.

"Oncologist?" We both stared at Dr. Clayton, then Dr. Barber, waiting for her to tell us what she thought was going on. She was clearly struggling to find the right words.

"Well, we're not exactly sure, but it looks like you might have leukemia. But . . ."

"*Leukemia?*" Jane interrupted before I could open my mouth to do the same. "How can that be?"

"As I said, we're not sure. That's why we need to talk to the oncologist and watch you for a few days," Dr. Barber said.

Jane was shaking her head, her eyes were filling, and she was gripping my hand hard. She had put her phone down to cover her eyes. "How can that be? I don't feel sick. Maybe a little tired. I had two miscarriages over the last six months. Could it be that?"

"Again, we're not sure. There's a flu going around, but you don't seem to have any flu symptoms," Dr. Clayton said.

Jane tried to cover her face, but she was sobbing now. I held her hand even tighter. The bile in my stomach was rising to my throat, and my chest was starting to tighten. I was in shock, but then felt a wave of nausea. Jane's words of protest and disbelief echoed in my head. *How could this be? Leukemia? No. She felt fine.*

I looked back toward the doctors, and my questions flew out fast and furious. I gave them no time to answer. "So, what are the next steps on this? What tests do we have to do? When can we figure this out? When will the oncologist see her? Will she be moved out of the ER?" Twenty questions mode is my default when I'm scared. That was all I could do to keep my shit together. The shock was like an ocean wave springing up out of nowhere and dragging me out to sea with it. I felt helpless struggling against the stinging wave of questions, fear, and doubts, and my Walnut Creek double espresso threatened to exit my mouth.

Dr. Clayton smiled sympathetically. "We're going to get her a room in the next couple of hours, Mr. Bolander. Then we'll get the oncologist to do a bone marrow biopsy. Since it's the weekend, she'll have to stay a couple of days so we can observe her."

I repeated the words in my head, trying to understand: *Observe her? A couple of days? Bone marrow biopsy?* It was all so overwhelming. I latched onto the idea that this had to be a mistake, that she had some nasty flu. *People Jane's age don't get leukemia. That's a kid's disease, isn't it?*

"We'll check back in on you guys in an hour or so. By then, we'll have a better idea and a plan." Dr. Clayton's eyes now told the whole story. She knew Jane had leukemia. She just didn't want to be the one to give us the news.

The two doctors left, and Jane and I sat there staring at each other. Tears welled up in both our eyes. There went our dinner plans and my relaxing weekend.

I was struggling to make some sense of what we'd heard. Leukemia. A blood disease. I'd helped raise money for Team In Training back in 2006. I'd lost an elementary school friend to leukemia. Scott had died when he was ten years old. I felt sick again. The lump in my stomach bobbed like a dingy about to be hit by a squall.

"Maybe it's just the flu. It's been going around," I said.

"Maybe. You need to call my parents. The reception is shitty here. Can you go do that?" Jane had wiped her tears and the gears in her brain were spinning, as were mine. Problem-solving mode engaged.

"Sure," I said, glad to have a concrete assignment. "I'll step out and do that. Don't worry. We're in the right place, you're safe, and we'll figure this all out." I kissed her forehead and gave her the best smile I could muster.

I walked outside into brisk late December air, feeling unsteady, as if I were a little drunk and about to feel the delayed effects of one more shot. *Leukemia. Holy fuck. This can't be happening.* I started to well up with emotion—another wave crashing over me. The tears stung my eyes as they dried in the chilly air. I stared at my phone with Tim's number queued up, ready to dial. I could feel the failure lump swell in my throat. My whole body was tense and my foot was tapping. I took deep breaths, but they didn't calm me down; they just made me dizzy. My nose started to run. My hand shook.

How the hell was I going to tell her parents?

Jane's dad, Tim, her mom, Emily, and her younger brother, Eric, took about forty-five minutes to get to the ER. On the phone, Tim asked me so many questions I could not answer. We'd agreed it was better for them to come to the ER so we could all plan how to handle things together.

By the time her family arrived, Jane had seen the on-call oncologist, and they were preparing to move her to a regular room in the hospital. She'd be in the cardiac ward because there were no beds in the cancer ward.

Cancer ward. Yesterday we were in Walnut Creek celebrating Christmas, and today we're all crammed into the hospital and Jane might have leukemia. Are we being punked?

The oncologist confirmed the possibility of leukemia, but to be sure he had to do a bone marrow biopsy, something that would happen after Jane was in her hospital room.

The plan we'd come up with, if you could call it that, was for me to go back to our apartment to gather up enough clothes for both of us for a three- or four-day stay. Jane's parents and brother would travel back and forth to Walnut Creek to bring us food and spend some time with Jane so I could do other things, like figure out how I was going to keep my shit together.

The torrent of texts and calls came fast and furious. It seemed like just as I got a handle on returning Phil's call or texting back Ria or getting off the phone with my parents, there would be nothing more than a brief pause, never enough to catch my breath, and then the torrent would start again.

The repetition and confusion of who I'd told what and when made me second-guess myself. *Do I need to call Sarah back? Didn't I just do that?* The blur of it all was made more frustrating by not knowing any answers, like what the prognosis was, or how to answer the response that most broke my heart: "Oh no. That can't be. How's she doing?" I actually never thought to ask her how she was doing, or rather we were too busy trying to figure out what to do to consider how either of us was doing.

WHEN MONDAY MORNING FINALLY ROLLED around, Jane was assigned an oncologist, Dr. Lee.

"Mrs. Bolander. We looked at the results," Dr. Lee said.

"Please, call me Jane. Mrs. Bolander sounds so old. I'm only thirty-five"

"Okay. Jane." He smiled gently. "We took a look at the bone marrow biopsy, and we have confirmed that it's leukemia. Acute myeloid leukemia, or AML, to be exact."

Jane started to cry. I followed her lead as she clenched my hand. Dr. Lee had kind eyes and a compassionate voice. He must have delivered the same speech to dozens of patients and knew the weight of his words.

"I know this is scary. Do you need a minute?"

"No. No. I'm fine." Jane took a deep breath and wiped her eyes. I tried to do the same. "So, what's the plan?" she asked.

"Well, you'll need chemotherapy. The sooner, the better. We're not sure of the exact type of AML you have. We're sending out a sample for DNA sequencing, but either way, you're going to need what's called induction chemotherapy. We'd like to start that right away."

"I read that chemo makes you sterile. Is that true?" We'd read up on the likely treatment options over the weekend, and all were caustic, with horrible side effects. It seemed they would all make you sterile, or rather, put you into early menopause.

"I'm afraid it does. I saw from your records that you've had two miscarriages over the past six months."

"Yes. We are trying to have kids and we're looking into IVF."

"Well, I'll give you some info about a doctor at UCSF who does cancer fertility treatment. Your best bet is to harvest your eggs before chemo. We can coordinate that with them." Dr. Lee was clearly trying to give us some encouragement. He paused to let it all sink in, but it was going to take more than a pause. He reached over and took Jane's other hand. "I know this is a lot to take in. We'll make sure you are safe and have all the information you need." He shook my hand and left.

CHAPTER 2

A Beautiful Accident

When I first met Jane, I had been separated from Margaret for six months and had just turned forty that February. To deal with the pain of being that year's "50 percent of marriages fail" statistic even though we'd made it eighteen years, ten as husband and wife, I drank more than usual.

It was June 2012, and I was attending my first Alice B. Toklas Pride Breakfast, and everyone seemed to be particularly happy. The Ninth Circuit had just ruled that California's Prop 8 was unconstitutional. Yank Sing on Spear Street was full of love and excitement about the future. I was not in the mood for either, but I showed up to this 8 a.m. Sunday brunch lovefest to support my new friend London Breed's race for District 5 supervisor.

What struck me about Jane was her long black hair that brushed the small of her back as it glistened in the morning light and her beautiful smile, big brown eyes, and a Cindy Crawford–style beauty mark that, I found out later, was considered lucky in her Asian heritage. Specifically, Jane was first-generation Taiwanese, and even more specifically, Hakka, a people who migrated from the mountains of mainland China to what was called Isla Formosa, meaning "beautiful island," named by the Portuguese in the 1500s. Most people know Taiwan as a place where bubble tea comes from, or as the place that Chiang Kai-shek fled to after being thrown out of China by Mao Zedong (also known as Chairman Mao) during the Cultural Revolution. Jane's ancestors predated that migration.

It was not love at first sight. I was a little smitten but was not in a situation where I could imagine someone like Jane would be interested in me. I was a broken man filled with a rage that drove me ever harder to wake up at 5 a.m. to swim, bike, or run to near exhaustion for an Ironman I was training for.

How could someone like Jane want to be with someone like me?

But I was wrong. Jane saw the goodness and potential in people—even me. She had a knack for making people feel special in a way that was not too much or too little. She made people feel heard, and when they did not reciprocate, they'd get an earful. I noticed this almost immediately with her. Her laugh was infectious, her smile stunning. Later, once I knew her better, her friends often remarked that her eyes could look deep into your soul and rattle your heart with the notion that you, and only you, mattered to her in that moment.

She was quick to praise but equally quick to call people out on their bullshit. On our fifth date, she announced before dessert that if I did not want kids, we should just end it and not waste each other's time.

For a month afterward, the topic of kids took up the better part of my therapy sessions.

Assertive yet compromising. Available yet reserved. Loving yet stern. Jane had all the characteristics I lacked and wanted to develop.

Although we didn't know it at the time, our love affair started the day after we met. She beat me to the punch and emailed right away. We did a whiskey fundraiser together three weeks after we met, which turned out to be a huge success and led to our first official fight. After four months, I was going to all her PR events to help out, and she was giving me support for my start-up.

When we started to talk about marriage, about a year and a half after that first meeting, Jane set up a time to meet her parents, in the most Jane way possible—at a pop-up restaurant in Oakland for her friend Pinky Cooper of Pinx Catering. Jane had helped Pinky through the food entrepreneurship nonprofit La Cocina, and they'd remained close. Jane was a volunteer at La Cocina, and she would teach the food entrepreneurs, all women of color, about the power of promotion, PR, and storytelling.

Jane also orchestrated the time and setting when I asked Tim for her hand in marriage on a crisp mid-January day in 2014. She made reservations at a downtown Walnut Creek Japanese restaurant that was early enough to beat the lunch rush and nice enough to give us some privacy. She coached me through it, telling me to call him Dr. Yin, to be myself and respectful but not too much of a kiss-up. The truth was, I was in awe of her father's accomplishments, including his PhD in chemistry.

This was only the fourth time I had met him and the first time we'd ever been alone. When I led with my rehearsed line, "Thank you for taking the time to meet, Dr. Yin," he stopped me and said, "No problem. And you can call me Tim."

"Um. Yeah. Okay," I said, looking down at the menu, still nervous.

Tim had an easy smile, like Jane's. She'd also gotten her round head and kind eyes from him. As we both got more comfortable, I realized Tim was almost as easy to talk to as Jane, and we discussed all sorts of things—my family, where I went to school, my start-up, and his import business. I still wasn't sure how to ask the big question, but within a few minutes, I knew I liked Jane's dad a lot. Eventually, the topic of marriage came up naturally as we were finishing lunch— and I had my opening.

"So, Dr. Yin—I mean, Tim," I stumbled. "Jane and I have known each other for a year and a half now, and we care deeply about each other. We're talking about getting married, but before I ask her, I wanted to talk to you first."

Whew. I'd gotten it out with minimal stuttering.

"Yes, Jane has told me about this possibility. I appreciate you asking me about this." He paused and looked at me across the table, his eyes steady and calm.

I thought he was waiting for more from me, so I jumped in, "Of course. For sure. If you have any questions or anything—you know, about my past marriage? I know that's not ideal. It was a tough situation." Thinking about Margaret still made a failure lump rise in my throat—and this time it tasted like the sashimi we'd had for lunch.

Tim smiled. "Yes, she told me about that. That's the past. I trust Jane's judgment. Ultimately, it's up to her to choose whom she wants to marry. I just want her to be happy."

"Me too. I want Jane to be happy too—and for a long, long time. She's so great, and I know I'm lucky to have met her. I would really like to ask her to marry me—if that's okay with you?"

"Yes, yes, of course." Tim leaned forward and broadened his smile so he looked even more like Jane. Then, in a lower tone, as if we were now members of the same club, he added, "I'm glad you asked me, but Jane always makes up her own mind, as you know. I trust her judgment and yours."

We got engaged on Valentine's Day 2014, my birthday. We married that October at Hamlin Mansion, four blocks away from Jane's apartment in Pacific Heights, which we'd decided would be our newlywed home until we started a family.

From: Jarie Bolander
Date: December 30, 2015
Subject: Welcome to Jane's Care Circle
To: janes-care-circle ▼

Thanks for all your messages of support and caring. It means a lot to Jane and the family.

You may be wondering what a Care Circle is. It's a place where we can share information about Jane's AML (acute myeloid leukemia) treatment and how she is doing. We borrowed this concept from a friend of mine who had to deal with a similar situation.

The idea will be to post as frequently as we get updates and to coordinate things such as ways you can help Jane out.

One thing to note about AML is that it does not have the classic stages that other cancers have. Rather, it has types based on blood cell counts and the accumulation of cells in other organs. At this point, it is unclear which type Jane has.

The treatment for AML is usually chemotherapy. We are not exactly sure which protocol she will be given, but what we've been told is to expect an initial three weeks in a hospital treatment protocol followed by several outpatient chemotherapy treatments depending on the outcome of the first round.

The problem with chemo is that it affects fertility, which launched off the other part of this saga—IVF.

In cases like Jane's, doctors advise patients to harvest and freeze off embryos because the risk of becoming infertile is really high. The complication with all this is that in order to do the IVF protocol (a pleasant ten-to-twelve-day regimen of belly fat hormone injections), you cannot be on chemo.

We are now staying at Jane's parents' house and are feeling all the love and support here. Jane's mom is diligently preparing delicious combinations of all the most nutritious foods, from seaweed soups to rice porridge concoctions.

Stay tuned for additional updates as we get them.
Thanks for your love and support,
Team Jane

CHAPTER 3

I Love It When a
Plan Comes Together

After absorbing the shock of Jane's diagnosis, we did what we always did when faced with a challenge: we organized. There was a ton of stuff to do, including arranging IVF at UCSF, letting friends and family know, preparing for the first round of chemo, and for me, taking over Jane's business, JSY PR & Marketing.

Yes, I was going to become a PR rep for professional athletes, start-ups, and nonprofits, because that was the only way we could support ourselves. My start-up was not paying me, and running JSY also gave me the flexibility to serve as a full-time caregiver.

If you had asked me six months, a year, or ten years earlier what I would be doing for work, the absolute last thing I would have suggested—other than maybe being a surgeon—was a job as a PR maven. I actually had no idea what Jane did other than yell at people on the phone at all hours of the day and night, complain about reporters, text on her Blackberry, and bang out email after email after email. She had a couple of interns who helped her out, but she liked to be in control and could never figure out why everyone else didn't work as fast and efficiently as she did or meet her high standards.

"So, what exactly do I have to do for the press conference for the No Traffick Ahead client?" I was sitting on her parents' living room couch taking notes. We had been there for less than a week after Jane's diagnosis, and I was still getting a download on all her clients. The most pressing one was No Traffick Ahead, a coalition of Bay Area anti–human trafficking groups. They had hired Jane to do public relations for their Super Bowl 50 campaign to raise awareness about human labor and sex trafficking.

"You need to figure out where to have it, get the media there, and do the press release. You have to coordinate with Betty Anne and find spokespeople for the movement." Jane was rattling off a laundry list that I was frantically scribbling down.

"Do you have a checklist or templates for this stuff?" I asked as I looked at the tasks I had zero idea how to accomplish.

"I have old emails and some email templates that I'll forward to you. Don't worry about that. I can help with that. What you really need to do is make sure the press shows up to cover it."

"Press. Okay. Like the nightly news? ABC, CBS, NBC? Like Cheryl Jennings, Dan Rather–type of nightly news?"

"Yeah, and the *Chron*, *Examiner*, and everyone else that's covering the Super Bowl in print and online. I have a list." Jane was still working as if she didn't have a life-threatening disease. "I can help while doing chemo. I just need you to be the point of contact. You know, the lead, the spokesman. I'll be behind the scenes."

"Okay. I guess." I shook my head as I stared at the notes again and sighed, "It's so overwhelming. I'm freaking out about this. I have no idea what I'm doing." The truth was, I was freaking out about *everything*: chemo, stepping away from my start-up, our future, and working with her clients. I had been to a lot of events with Jane, but always as her plus-one—never the person running the show.

"You'll be fine. As I said, I'll handle a lot of it. I just need you to go to the meetings and be the spokesman." Jane was typing an email, letting all her clients know about the new arrangement.

As she finished the email, she looked up at me and said, "I know this is a lot. Don't worry about it. Everyone loves talking to you, and you're really good at making people feel special. Just listen, smile, and make sure you remember everyone's name."

That made me feel a little bit better but did not push the failure lump back down. I'd have to take her word for it and do the best I could.

She wanted to help as much as possible, but it became clear within a few weeks that her full-time job was going to be getting better. Mine was making sure everything in the health-care obstacle course—doctor appointments, medications, paying bills, keeping up with her treatments, and being her advocate—happened as it should. The organs of health care need constant care and feeding.

I was also anointed JSY PR & Marketing partner/spokesman/CEO/Grand Poobah. I started to vape more and more. I chose vaping over drinking, edibles, and tinctures, since it was a lot easier to get the dose right. Edibles took thirty to forty-five minutes to kick in, lasted a lot longer, and made me a bit more paranoid. I attributed the paranoia to getting the wrong strain and the CBD to THC ratios being off—CBD being the "body high" and THC being the "head high." To relax, it's best to have more CBD.

Tinctures worked okay, but I could never keep the drops under my tongue for longer than a minute. It was also hard to talk with four to five drops of dirty-green slime under your tongue. Drinking had the standard and customary downsides.

After some experimentation, I settled on a 3:1 CBD to THC blend to relax my tense body and calm my racing mind. Two to three puffs was all it took. I could duck out quickly and not come back smelling like I was sprayed by a skunk. Remaining calm was important now that I had two full-time jobs, both of which I had no idea how to do.

ONE THING THAT HAD BECOME CLEAR RIGHT away was that we needed a communications plan. The first weeks were overwhelming with all the incoming emails, phone calls, and texts asking about Jane and what everyone could do to help. It was amazing how much coordination had to take place when someone got sick. I found myself repeating details and updates pretty much all day long. We needed a way to manage all the information, which was how we started using "Care Circle" emails. The idea came from my good friend Troy, one of about a dozen like-minded people who worked out together training for extreme endurance events, which was what this was feeling more and more like.

Jane and I awkwardly, but quickly, found our new normal. Gone were the fancy dinners, movie premieres, happy hours, dinners with friends, trips to Napa and Sonoma for wine tasting, the forty-first birthday wine and cheese surprise party she threw for me, and any kind of romance. Our lives now revolved around managing the chaos of treatments, JSY, and the most immediate task, IVF.

CHAPTER 4

The Right Stuff

The IVF process finished two days ahead of schedule. The two units of platelets were enough to prevent any complications, including internal bleeding, which is always a concern with AML patients since platelets are the glue that repairs the countless leaks in and out of our bodies. The whole IVF process was quick and painless for me. For Jane, it was a different story.

The ten-day sequence of hormone injections was easy after I figured out that doing them jab-to-the-heart *Pulp Fiction*–style was a mistake. I'd given Jane a big purple-yellow bruise on her stomach with the first injection, which spread out and lingered for the duration of her injections—a reminder that there was a good reason I was not a doctor.

USCF had a clinic that specialized in IVF for cancer patients. It was the best in the country for off-menstrual-cycle egg harvesting when you couldn't afford to wait. Tim drove us to the appointment and waited with us to see if the injections would produce enough eggs and if I had the right stuff on my end. Tim and I sat in the waiting room and listened to romantic Muzak piped in, which set the mood just right. I recognized

Peter Cetera's "The Next Time I Fall," which brought back awkward high school prom slow dance memories. That was followed by "Memories," by Babs herself.

Once we got into the organs of a health-care system, the challenges of boredom were many. It was a complex game of whack-a-mole sprinkled with waiting room after waiting room. Finally, when something did happen, my brain got overwhelmed with what sounded like the grown-ups in a Peanuts movie—*Wah waah wah waaah*. Taking notes felt futile, since I'd never be able to spell any of the twenty-five-cent words anyway, and yet I had to, since I'd never remember otherwise. That was why it was best to have at least one other person around to fill in the gaps postgame back in the locker room—hence Tim coming along to our appointment.

Jane was in a sedative haze in the recovery room after egg harvesting, and clearly judgment-impaired when she suggested, "We should do the surrogate when I'm going through chemo. That way, once I'm better, we'll have the baby."

"Let's not worry about that for now," I said. "We need to focus on one thing at a time." But I was actually thinking: *There's no fucking way I'm going to get a surrogate. I can't handle a wife recovering from cancer and a newborn at the same time. I can't even handle my two new jobs.* I had barely survived the first three weeks working at JSY and coordinating Jane's care, let alone the IVF injections and Care Circle updates. *Fucking no way, with a capital F.*

"Okay, but I want to start thinking about it," she insisted. "We can talk to Matt and Jeff about the process. Once I'm better, we should get going on that."

I should have expected this from Jane. She always wanted to get ahead of the curve, never working at a leisurely pace to check things off her infinite to-do list. Our friends Matt and Jeff had twins using a surrogate, so of course she'd want to get their input. Given her dire situation, I was proud that she wanted to plan for the future, because it showed her will to survive. I knew I'd have to talk her out of this particular plan as gently as possible.

"First, let's get through the chemo," I repeated, "and then we can plan. Plenty of time to sort things out. Let's focus on getting you cured. That's about all I can handle right now."

"What about JSY? We can't let that slip. I spent a lot of time building it—over ten years! It's my first baby. You have to promise me we'll keep it going." Jane was now frantic and agitated, struggling to sit up in bed but unable to move much due to the pain of the procedure.

"I already said I would," I said a little more harshly than was necessary. I should have realized her agitation was her way of dealing with the emotional stress of what she was going through. But her way of piling things on had been overwhelming before her diagnosis. Now she wasn't capable of handling everything, and the pile-on was more than I could bear. "I told the guys at LSS that I can't be around right now, and I'm committed to JSY. But you and your health come first." My voice was as soft as I could possibly make it, but she knew me well enough to feel the strain, to detect the irritation.

"Promise me you'll keep it going. It's our *only* source of income, and I don't want to shut it down. *Promise me, babe.*" She slurred her words as she fought the sedative and tried to sit up again but slid back down because of the pain.

We'd had this baby/business rope-a-dope discussion round after round for weeks before the IVF procedure. The business part always started with me asking a question since nothing was documented. No systems were in place. There was no *process* to help me figure out how to get the work done. All information about JSY was in Jane's head, or in hundreds of folders in her email inbox, something she was actually proud of. I knew an "all in my head" system was common practice for solo entrepreneurs, but that didn't help me sort out the mess. One time, I'd spent the better part of a day trying to sort out critical media contacts so I knew whom to email and how for the No Traffick Ahead press conference. By "sort," I mean reading through mega threads of emails that Jane forwarded me to find the single nugget of gold to cut and paste into a Google Sheet, hardly the high-tech engineering environment I was used to.

My failure lump threatened to suffocate me. My chest tightened. I tried to stay measured but failed. "I'm going to do the best I can, but we need to find some tools and get organized. It's too hard to ask you questions every five minutes."

"I don't want to spend money," she said. "If you can organize stuff for free, then do it. We just have to keep JSY going. I worked too hard to shut it down." Jane was becoming more emotional, anxious, and on the verge of tears, still exhausted from the procedure and irritated by her slow mind from the anesthesia. When she raised her voice, it triggered me to raise mine too.

"I'll do my best, but if I need to buy a tool to make things more efficient, I'm going to do it!"

A nurse glanced over from the other side of the room, raising her index finger to her lips in an effort to quiet us down.

"You always waste money on things we don't need," Jane shot back in a whisper. The sedative was starting to wear off too soon, in my opinion.

"C'mon. That's not fair. If you want me to do this, I need to make some decisions and get organized. It's overwhelming. I don't think like you do."

"Overwhelming? Who is the one with cancer? Me. I'm the one who's overwhelmed. All you have to do is what I say." Jane's tone was harsh and dictatorial. She loved micromanaging, and I hated being micromanaged. I knew this was all coming from her feeling overwhelmed and out of control, so all I could do was try to shut the conversation down.

"Whatever. Let's not talk about this now. We're at the hospital," I mumbled with my voice and head lowered.

"Don't buy anything without asking me first. Promise," she said.

"Okay. I promise," I agreed, feeling defeated, the full lump now in my throat. Better to just agree than keep fighting, I figured. We'd have plenty more to fight about later.

THE CAR RIDE BACK TO JANE'S PARENTS' house was quiet, as usual after an argument. I kept ruminating over what she'd said, which kept the failure lump firmly lodged halfway up my windpipe. Jane broke the silence when we reached Walnut Creek and were unpacking our things in her childhood room.

"Babe, I'm sorry I second-guessed your judgment. If you need to buy something, go ahead. You're now the CEO, and it's up to you." She gave me a big hug.

"You know I'm not going to buy something we don't need. I'll run things by you first. I really need to get a handle on this. It's making me mental." I was so glad she had seen it my way. More stress was the last thing we needed right now.

"I know. I'll help all I can before chemo. We can go through the clients and come up with a game plan. I'm happy you're running JSY."

As she pulled away, I saw a new concern in her eyes I hadn't seen before. JSY really was her first baby, and she didn't like leaving it in someone else's hands—not even mine.

CHAPTER 5

We'll Figure It Out

The second miscarriage put a strain on our relationship. It had happened right after our trip to Paris in October 2015, and four months after the first miscarriage. Jane and I had always been open with each other, but it was so hard to talk about losing two babies. I had no idea what to say. The Internet was no help. All the advice was basically, "Everything will be okay. Just keep trying." The only thing that helped was talking to friends about their miscarriages—that made us both feel less alone.

We had first realized the value of talking things through during couples therapy, which I had vowed to do if I ever got serious with anyone else after Margaret. Our six sessions with a therapist six months into our relationship set up a foundation for learning about each other and sorting out our differences so we could build on a solid foundation of understanding going forward.

Our therapist, Evette, got right down to business as Jane and I took our seats in the converted three-floor Victorian flat that housed marriage and family therapists (MFT). Jane was frustrated by how I handled social situations and my hesitation about having kids.

"So, what are you two here about?" Evette asked, opening up her notebook.

"I was married before and want to explore the best way to communicate in this new relationship," I said.

"Jarie wanted me to come. I want to know why he doesn't talk to me," Jane answered with her usual bluntness. Evette's eyes widened a bit as she took down some notes.

It was the first minute of the first session, and we were already getting into it.

"I talk to you all the time. What does that even mean?" I could hear the defensiveness in my voice but couldn't stop it.

"I always have to start. You just sit there. Like a lump. You talk to plenty of random people, but never me. Why is that?"

"You wait till I'm about to go to sleep, or worse, after we come back from some event. I'm drained. When I get home, I just want to crash."

Evette listened and scribbled as we bickered back and forth for what felt like twenty minutes. Every time Jane criticized me, I felt the familiar lump of failure swell and bob up and down in my throat—the same feeling I'd gotten when Margaret gave me the silent treatment or when I sensed she was frustrated with me.

Along with the lump, I could feel cortisol building up from the pit of my stomach, tightening my chest and making my nose run. A surge of nervous energy bounced my leg up and down. I got that same feeling around large groups of people or whenever I faced a stressful situation. My adrenaline always surged in response to the nerves. The worst part was the crash after the adrenaline. That was why I was always so tired after stressful meetings or big social gatherings. When it was particularly bad, I'd get a massive headache and become narcoleptic as soon as I felt I was in a safe place.

Finally, Evette interrupted us, "It sounds to me like Jarie gets drained by social engagements, while you, Jane, get energized. Did I get that right?"

Jane nodded. "I love to come home and talk about the night. It's great to relive the evening to decompress."

"To me, that's torture. I just want to forget about it," I piped in. I'd pushed down the failure lump enough to speak in a more subdued, reasonable tone, trying to bob and weave around it.

"Jarie, it does sound like you don't mind having a conversation with random people at a party, but not with Jane. Why do you do that?" Evette said.

"I get nervous and want people to find me interesting. I try really hard to make a good impression." Actually, I wanted people to love me, but I didn't have the courage to say that out loud.

"I see. Can you see how that makes Jane angry? She sees what she wants given to other people." Evette wasted no time in getting to the heart of the matter. The lump made it back to my throat along with more cortisol and a rumble in my stomach. My leg bounced even more.

"Yeah, I guess so. How am I supposed to deal with it then? I get so nervous around other people, especially strangers, that I just start talking." I looked down at my shoes, embarrassed.

Evette thought for a moment and suggested, "Why don't you save some energy for Jane? Limit your interactions. Maybe leave earlier so it's not so draining?"

She had a point. Why waste my energy on random people when chatting about our day meant so much to Jane?

"I can give that a try." I nodded and felt the failure lump retreat. Jane smiled her approval.

The rest of our sessions were variations on the first, and by the end of them we both felt better about speaking our minds.

THE SAVING ENERGY IDEA MADE A BIG impact on our relationship. I no longer crashed out after a big event. I even started to enjoy the recap, like the time Jane threw a fundraiser for the Snow Foundation, a nonprofit formed by Jack, J.T., and

Stephanie Snow to find a cure for Wolfram syndrome, a rare degenerative genetic disease that Stephanie's daughter, Raquel, had been diagnosed with in 2010.

My strategy to "save some for Jane" at these kinds of events was twofold and did not rely on us leaving early. The first step was to get a job where I could ignore people or could easily say, "Excuse me, I need to take care of something." The second step was to hide out and decompress as soon as my assignment was done. This worked perfectly at the Snowman Classic.

"Did you see all those cougars going after the young players? It was like a feeding frenzy," Jane said, excited to see how I felt about the drama.

We had just gotten back to our apartment after the event, a celebrity cocktail competition to raise money for the foundation. Jane had spent months planning it and coordinating with the San Francisco Giants, J.T.'s former team, celebrity chef Ryan Scott, and the two hundred–plus guests who had paid to see the best mixologists in the city.

"I never knew that stuff happened to players." I was naive about the sports world. Jane had assigned me to watch over Hunter Pence and some other guys, basically making sure no one bugged them. But the onslaught of women was crushing, and it was hard to pull them away. I was shocked at how bold some of the women were, and at what they were wearing. It was *RuPaul's Drag Race* meets *The Real Housewives of Orange County*.

"You should have seen what happened when we went to the club with Amar'e. It was even more insane. The women *flooded* in. I had to make sure we got seated in the VIP section or bring in some sort of security. And the outfits! You'd think they couldn't wear much less, but then, *boom*, another one shows up in barely a thong."

Jane loved to tell stories about her early days in LA as a publicist for professional athletes, and I loved to hear about her adventures. I could see what our therapist had meant about recapping the night and how it energized Jane. It even started to sometimes energize me because I was making a conscious effort to save social time for Jane.

"Thanks, Babesteins, for helping tonight. It was really nice of you to do it. It makes me so happy to see you in the mix, even though I know you don't like it so much." Jane was always thankful when I helped her out. And helping made me feel needed and loved.

"Of course," I said. "Ride or die. Remember? Besides, when I become a famous author, you'll be throwing parties like that for me. I only hope you'll provide muscle as good as me to protect me from all my fans." I started to chuckle. The idea was ridiculous, but the allure of being important and in the mix did feel good, especially when I knew that Jane would have my back.

Jane was the one who'd first brought up the idea of ride or die. Originally, it was some sort of motorcycle riding thing, like you'd rather die if you could not ride your bike. Hip-hop had taken it over to mean that a woman would ride till the end with her man, no matter what he did. Nowadays, it means either a man or a woman who will go to the very end for their partner—no matter what happens.

"Babe! You'd hate that. I think it's the other way around—*I'll* become a famous author after I publish all the crazy things I have seen in this business. It's going to be a huge bestseller."

"Yeah, you're probably right. I'm exhausted already."

"Me too, let's go to bed."

CHAPTER 6

Rules of the Road

Hospitals always gave a specific time to check in, and the room was never ready. Jane and I showed up on time for once to a depressing, slit-windowed basement room with droning Muzak and a view looking up toward Geary Street with dozens of legs of all shapes and sizes strolling by. Time slowed down in hospitals. They were the worst combination of hurry up and wait mixed with a this-is-always-how-we-do-it attitude.

It had been a couple of days since the egg harvest, fertilization of five eggs, and our fight about how I would manage JSY. As the next part of our leukemia journey began, I felt my failure lump rising from my stomach, slowly tightening in my chest like a coiling python on its way to a permanent home in my throat, triggered all the more by my hatred of hospital smells.

My whole body clenched up when I passed the threshold into the wet stickiness of sickness, hand sanitizer, and disinfectant that hung in the air like the moldy patchouli incense in a head shop on the Haight. This smell combined with the wait got my leg bouncing at such a rate that people stared at me with that awkward "Are you going to stop doing that?" look.

We eventually made it to our assigned room where the first order of business was unpacking Jane's Cancer-Fighting Kit. We'd assembled the kit with help from Google and several wise friends, and I schlepped it around in a custom monogrammed *Team Jane* canvas bag about the size of those blue Ikea shopping bags. It included the following:

- a warm, comfy pink bathrobe that The Dude himself would have envied
- a pair of wool-lined moccasin slippers
- comfy, oversized clothes with elastic waistbands and minimal snaps
- pink heart-shaped Post-it Notes for decorating the cream-and-mellow-yellow-colored hospital room
- a Germ Terminator dual toothbrush sanitizer
- enough Endure 300 hand sanitizer to last a year
- assorted crackers, nuts, and candies
- a corkboard covered with pictures of friends and family
- chargers for electronics too numerous to admit to
- cannabis-derived products, also too numerous to admit to

As I unpacked and sorted, I was struck by how quickly our relationship had morphed into something new. The kit was one part of that. Before Jane got sick, we were a type A power couple, conquering the world together. Now I was the designated care-giver, and Jane was the dependent who relied on me for physical and emotional support. I had to be her caregiver and advocate. Her family would help in any way they could, and mine would offer to help, but I was captain of Team Jane with a singular goal: to make sure we didn't lose the MVP.

The dynamics of our new relationship became clear when Jane had her peripherally inserted central catheter (PICC) line installed. PICC lines are semi-permanent IVs that snake their way from your arm into your heart. They are better than a traditional central line, which is placed over the chest, close to the heart, because a PICC is easier to cover and move around with. Jane would have to be connected to an infusion pump for the duration of her chemo treatment, so she appreciated anything that made it easier.

At 6 p.m. on the first day with the PICC, Jane got up and asked, "Babe, can you help me cover the PICC line? The nurses are taking forever. I feel gross and need to take a shower." She was holding her arms out like a marionette being moved around by an invisible puppeteer so that the tubing would not get caught on her ill-fitting pale blue hospital gown and her His & Hers sweatpants. We had not yet figured out how to tame the air conditioner/heater that rumbled and rattled on and off all day, so sweatpants were essential, along with my zip-up hoodie.

I looked up from my laptop, trying to understand the problem. "How are we supposed to do that?"

"I bought a sleeve. I just need help putting it on. Also, can you get fresh towels? We need to make sure everything is super clean. I don't want to get an infection. Fresh towels every day. Got it?" Jane's voice rose impatiently, a little louder with each sentence.

"Do I ask the nurse or ring the bell, or what?" This was my first overnight stay in a hospital since the day I was born (on the same floor of the same hospital forty-five years earlier, oddly enough).

"Just go ask the nurse. I'm sure they have a huge stash somewhere." Jane was visibly irritated as she slowly looked around, trying to figure out how to take off her gown without twisting, getting the dual six-inch dangling leads of the PICC line caught on her clothes and the hospital bed.

I wasn't good at making requests to anyone about anything, let alone hospital staff. Despite the check-in delay and weird smells, I still thought we were in a kind of hotel with special amenities where the staff would provide all we needed. As it turned out, it was nothing like a hotel.

Our new home was in what they called Six South on 2425 Geary Boulevard in San Francisco. Our view out the window was a roof covered with HVAC machines and ducting to take said heated and conditioned air to our room. Standing on my tiptoes, I could see the City Center mall to the west.

Just outside the door to the right was a long corridor and a window looking east toward San Francisco Bay. The nurses' station was to the left, with a hallway leading to the maternity ward where I was born and another hallway toward Six West, reserved for stroke patients. To get to Six West, you walked past the public bathrooms and five elevators—two for patients only and three for visitors. The door to the stairwell was the farthest point north. I thought my best bet for the towels would be to ask a nurse or orderly, but at that moment what we soon came to know as the 6 p.m. chow bell chaos was in full swing. Infusion pumps beeped. Patients moaned. Call buttons dinged. Microwave fans whirred and strained under the pressure of heating dinner for two dozen patients who needed to eat, apparently at the same time.

Beep. Moan. Ding. Whir. Repeat. I wandered around doe-eyed trying to make eye contact. How was I supposed to get anyone's attention? I swerved to avoid bumping into a nurse in well-pressed scrubs who sternly looked at me and asked me what I wanted. She quickly headed to a full laundry cart and returned with exactly what Jane needed.

"What took you so long? It's only towels." Jane was back in bed, watching *Blue Bloods* on her computer and frowning when I returned from the quest.

"I know, but it's crazy out there."

"They don't just have a stack of towels you can grab?"

"This is not the pool at the Ritz. Do you know how many patients are on this floor? It's hard to get the nurses' attention."

Her face softened, and she grinned. I think she liked the comparison to the Ritz.

"Yeah, I know," she said. "Did you hear that guy moaning? What's up with that?"

"He's an old guy who fell and broke his hip. The nurses were helping him get up, and he was *not* happy about it."

"Oh, that must have been painful." There was real sympathy in her voice, then a return to practical matters. "I guess we should make sure we have a ton of extra towels. I want to take a shower every day."

"Got it. Anything else?" I had picked up a pen and a stack of pink heart-shaped Post-its and was ready to take orders from my charge.

"Make sure we have plenty of cups. It's important not to have dirty ones lying around. And I'll need that gentle soap. And more sweats. And more hugs." Jane smiled as I looked up from the list I was scribbling on.

I leaned over the hospital bed and gave her a big hug, careful not to disrupt the newly inserted PICC line. "Hugs-a-plenty. I got that. Towels—not so much."

From: Jane Bolander
Date: January 20, 2016 at 11:22 a.m.
Subject: Day One Chemo Jitters
To: janes-care-circle ▼

I had very little knowledge about chemotherapy or all the various cancers out there. I just knew that all those words—chemo, leukemia, and cancer—have an awful and scary connotation. Without cancer in my family history and being a healthy person below age thirty-five, it seemed like something so far away from my own life, something only other people experienced.

At 8 p.m., it was a total trip to see the bags o' chemo come from the pharmacy. The harsh med (my emails won't contain fancy proper terminology like Jarie's) is red, and now my pee is all orange . . . it came through my system pretty much instantly! The trippy-ness is knowing these random bags of fluid are going to save my life!

I also had a PICC line put into a "nice, juicy vein," per the doc, which goes directly to my heart. That's an awesome tool because they can put meds in me and take blood out without having to "prick me twice" or fifty-plus times.

I was SUPER nervous before the chemo started running . . . probably the most nervous I've ever been in my life. NOTE TO SELF: Stop reading scary blogs, medical articles, Reddit posts, and news articles prior to chemo.

To combat the "losing my appetite" fears, I keep eating anytime I feel ANY sort of hunger. It's before 10 a.m. today, and I've had crackers, leftover dinner, breakfast, and a green smoothie. I may become the only person that gains a ton of weight after chemo . . . and I won't be complaining if that's the case!

Day 1 Overall Assessment: This chemo experience hasn't been that bad at all (SO FAR). I am constantly reminded by the professionals that every person's experience is different, but that doesn't stop me from asking everyone that walks into the room what's normal for me to feel about every five to ten minutes.

Overall Leukemia Diagnosis Assessment: Once you get diagnosed with something nasty, it seems to become your whole life, as well as the lives of those who love you. Sometimes when we drive to the hospital for a blood draw, I look at a restaurant and think, *Hey, if things were "normal" again, we would be planning a fun dinner there.* (Yes, back to the eating thing again.)

But honestly, I'm not thinking that it's unfair or something. I mean, if it's unfair, then does that mean it's fair that someone else has it? I think sometimes sh*t just happens to you, and that's pretty much it. The only way to deal with it is day by day, and don't push for any more than that.

I also look around the room at all the wonderful photos of friends and awesome care package gifts that have made this stay so cozy and will surely come to the rescue as time goes on. We were lauded by the staff for the cleanest room (yay!).

Jarie and I are also immensely grateful to my parents and brother for all the many meals, help with plans, drives to appointments, extra hugs, and so much more. I'm proud to have parents that don't let me wallow in self-pity and instead focus on staying mentally strong. That is where I have channeled the strength I need for this experience and all my life.

Thank you to my awesome hubby who encouraged us to start this Care Circle group per his friend Troy's advice. He's been such an incredible partner in crime during this experience and always. Sorry I wake you up so many times when I pee . . . haha.

He and Alena are also holding down the fort at JSY (along with other friends who have stepped up to help) during some crucial projects that we have going on, so my first "baby" can stay afloat. For that, I'm so grateful.

Love,
Jane

CHAPTER 7

It's Like It Won't Be Me

"Babesteins, people really read the Care Circle. How fun!" A smile spread over Jane's face as she looked over the responses on her laptop. It had been less than a day since she'd sent her update.

"I told you. People want to be involved. They love it, even more when you send out a note. Everyone wants to know how you're doing." I was on the foldout chair/bed tucked in the corner next to the bathroom, so that every time Jane got up during the night to pee, the door swung out and hit my dangling legs. I'd learned that if I vaped enough of my 3:1 CBD/THC mix I might not wake up, but some nights were better than others.

"Still. I can't believe people read the whole thing." In that little moment she looked like she used to, with a big smile that opened up her beautiful brown eyes, and was so giddy I thought she might jump up and do one of her song and dance routines. Usually, her expression was ponderous crossed with worry punctuated by a slight smirk when she was amused. It was great to see the Care Circle so supportive and her so happy.

The chemo had started, and our new normal was starting to sink in. *We might just make it through after all.*

By that point, I was working during the day at JSY down-town and coming back to the hospital at night to sleep in the room with Jane. Tim and Emily took turns during the day so that we had round-the-clock coverage.

Whenever I entered Jane's room after a day out in the real world, my failure lump always rose in my throat. I'd take a few long, deep breaths, trying to force down the lump as I applied the Ecolab gel hand sanitizer. That little breathing exercise sometimes helped with the lump and the tsunami of cortisol rushing through my veins. The outside world started to disappear on my ride up in the elevator and my slow walk to Jane's room. The smell of Band-Aids, microwaved cornbread chicken, and soiled linens wiped out everything else. My sick, frustrated, moody, bored wife would want me to talk to her, help her, and entertain her. I'd been on prison release for eight hours, and there was a price for that. While Jane was in a twelve-by-eight room being poked and prodded, listening to the moans and groans of people and machines, she looked forward to my return, and I didn't blame her. Meanwhile, I counted the hours before I could escape her room and go to my secret place.

I had discovered my secret place accidentally as I was wandering the building one day, looking for a quiet spot to make a phone call. The back stairs of our part of the hospital faced west, with a view of Geary Street toward the City Center mall, to the left, and Tony's Cable Car Restaurant, to the slight right, with its retro '50s neon sign welcoming tourists and locals to "Drive-In for Burgers, Shakes, Fries, and Hot Dogs."

My secret place was a six-by-six-foot landing with a stair-case leading to the ground level—a fire escape of some sort. It was open-air, covered only by black pigeon netting, so I could exhale my vape pen without getting caught.

Every evening I got Jane up to speed on what was happening at JSY, took a few laps with her around the sixth floor, infusion pump in tow, watched some TV, ate, and helped her shower. I then made my escape to the back stairs. For five to ten precious minutes, I took long drags of my vape pen, soaked in the night air, listened to the rumble of traffic on Geary, and stared at Tony's glowing sign. In those few minutes, I could calm down and vape the day away, finding a moment of peace, no matter how much stress had piled up in the previous twenty-four hours.

The stress took a lot of different forms, including a steep learning curve for all of us on Team Jane. For Jane, understanding the medical terminology and protocols got harder as the effects of chemo kicked in. We determined early on that at least one family member, if not two, had to be with her whenever she spoke to her doctors.

Jane's chemo protocol was known as "3 + 7." Daunorubicin for three days concurrently with cytarabine for seven days as a twenty-four-hour drip. Her total time on chemo was seven days, and after that week she would be monitored for seven to fourteen days to determine her response.

We were told that she wouldn't feel the effects until after the seven-day treatment was done because it would take that long for the drugs to work. During that period, we had to follow a strict protocol of handwashing, avoiding sick people, and getting ahead of any nausea or mouth sores with treatments. The rules were hard to remember, and even harder to implement.

"Hey, babe. Make sure you wash your hands. Were you around any sick people?" Jane would ask as I walked into the room after work. My backpack would still be hanging on my shoulder.

"I don't think so. Just the normal people on Muni." I'd put my bag down on a chair and move to the sink to wash my hands.

After a few times of doing this, she looked at me and asked, "Why don't you take an Uber or Lyft?"

"The stop is ten feet from this hospital, and it goes right by the office. It's kinda silly to Lyft."

"Muni is dirty, and if you get sick, that will be really bad. If you get sick, then what? Think about it. Then you won't be able to be with me," Jane pleaded, and started to cry—not something she did often. "I need you to stay healthy."

"All right. All right. I'll start taking Lyft. No Uber. I'm not a fan." She buried her head in my chest as I hugged her and eventually stopped crying.

"No more coffee either. It's dehydrating. You should drink more water." She was smiling again as she pulled away from me.

"Taking a Lyft? Yes. Give up coffee? Nope. I need it to function. More water? Sure. Deal?"

"Deal."

I counted that exchange as a little victory and savored it. I was also glad she had not asked about vaping.

As the number of nights spent at the hospital wore on, sleep deprivation, stress, and Jane's chemo brain were taking a toll. Not working out the way I used to was not helping.

Physical movement was the best stress relief and anti-depressant for me. Not being able to throw some weights around regularly created a situation where I could not down-regulate the repeated flood of cortisol and adrenaline that made me drink more double espressos and eat more frosted cranberry scones for ten seconds of dopamine bliss. Vaping temporarily numbed the stress, but never enough to fully make it go away. The world presented itself as a dreamlike haze that looked like when you opened your eyes in a pool. I struggled to wake up from it.

I was running Jane's company, managing her care, answering all sorts of questions from friends and family, and still trying to be of help with my own start-up. I could feel the strain in every part of my body, especially my throat, where the familiar failure lump pulsed like the coiling of a python as it smashed its prey. It only retreated away after three hits of my vape pen. Even then, the retreat only lasted what felt like the Green Mile back to Jane's room.

How was I going to make it through this?

CHAPTER 8

The Only Easy Day Was Yesterday

When I first met Jane, I was training for an Ironman. That Sunday morning, I had even dragged myself out of bed at 4:30 a.m. to do a six-mile training run in Golden Gate Park. Normally, I would have slept in, but the drive to get it done overwhelmed my hangover.

I had found endurance sports in high school when being on the cross-country team was required to try out for soccer. Cross-country was my first experience with how powerful the mind is when dealing with pain, suffering, and fatigue.

Coach Woodhall, or "Woody," as everyone called him, was the varsity soccer coach and, later on, the cross-country coach. He would run with us in the hills above Carlmont High School, which bordered San Carlos and my hometown of Belmont, thus the name. The hills and canyons around Carlmont were steep, poison oak–filled, single-track trails where generations of Carlmont cross-country and soccer teams built up endurance and grit to handle the challenges of the sport.

Woody's methodology was simple. We would do hill runs or repeats before we even touched a soccer ball. These runs would be three to four miles, broken up with group push-ups and sit-ups every half a mile or so. We all hated it but later realized that these runs before practice were meant to break us down physically so we could get used to playing while tired and bond as a team. While the hills built our endurance, Repeat Hill made us a team.

There is nothing like a shared grueling, even painful, experience to bond people together. Maybe it's the idea that everyone is equally miserable. Misery is what Repeat Hill was all about.

When I started training for an Ironman, I thought about Repeat Hill and Coach Woody often—how we'd end the hill run by stopping at the base of a 200-foot fire road right behind C-wing. This rutted, uneven stretch of dirt had a small plateau at the top and a narrow single-track trail that would bring you back down to the start. A repeat consisted of running up the hill and then down to the start. That would be one. We'd do five to ten of those depending on Woody's mood. In cases where he was annoyed that we were slacking, we'd have to carry one of our teammates up the hill. The usual order was the smaller guys would carry the bigger guys, then we'd switch at the bottom. If you were unlucky, you'd have to carry Woody, which was particularly hard given the slime sheen of sweat that covered his shirtless body. He was also at least 185 pounds of dense muscle. On more than one occasion, I almost dropped him due to my burning thighs, gasping breaths, and his ever-present voice yelling in my ear, "Hurry up, Bolander!"

The magical thing about endurance training was that any time you wanted to quit, you would immediately regret it or, after taking a brief rest, realize that your body had more in the tank. This was the state of mind I was in getting up at 4:30 a.m. the morning I met Jane—and also using physical training as my go-to stress relief.

I was three months out from my first Ironman in September of 2012 and training at least twenty hours a week, on top of having a full-time job. After successfully finishing the Ironman, I set my sights on a new challenge that was more team oriented as opposed to individual. That led me to multiday team endurance events, like the GORUCK Challenge and the Endeavor Team Challenge. These also gave me a sense of community and a set of friends that Jane always encouraged me to have.

From the get-go, Jane indulged me through all the training I was doing, but the ultimate test of that indulgence was Kokoro, a fifty-plus-hour endurance event that was based on Navy SEAL Hell Week. It was meant to test you in ways that you couldn't even fathom, let alone train for. Of course, there were physical standards to meet, like being able to do fifty push-ups, fifty sit-ups, fifty air squats, ten pull-ups, and run 1.5 miles in fewer than fourteen minutes in combat boots. The Kokoro game is all about the mental game of the unknown while you're sleep-deprived, hungry, dehydrated, and failing.

To an outsider, that a forty-three-year-old was doing Kokoro might have seemed extreme, but Jane knew that it was important for me to have a community of like-minded friends, only saying to me the day I left for Kokoro, "Babe. I know this is important to you, but please don't do anything stupid. If you have to quit, just quit."

"You know me. I'll be safe," I said as I packed up my red Mini Cooper for the over eight-hour drive to SEALFIT HQ in Encinitas, California, to start my Kokoro adventure.

"Yeah, but why do you have to do this? What do you have to prove? You're not going into the military or anything like that."

"I want to see what it's like and if I can do it. It's the ultimate challenge for me." The truth was I did have something to prove—both to myself and the little voice in my head that told me I was never good enough, smart enough, successful enough, or worthy enough for someone to love me. I wanted more than anything to prove to the world, and my dad, that I could handle myself in the most brutal of circumstances.

"Okay. Love you. Drive safe. Call me as soon as you're done," she said. I could tell she was worried but also that she loved me and wanted me to come back in one piece since it was only six months till our wedding in October.

I kept my promise and completed Kokoro that summer with minimal injuries and a new sense of the power of the mind and body. The lessons of Kokoro were many, but the one that would later burn in my brain was surf torture.

I wasn't exactly sure of the origins of surf torture, but every single Navy SEAL recruitment video had a sequence of a locked-arm protest line of candidates getting pounded by the surf. The application of surf torture was simple.

A line of candidates locked arms and walked toward the break line. The art in this was getting the position of the candidates just right—too far in, and the water was too deep; too close to the shore, and the waves didn't crash enough.

The multiple times we did this during Kokoro, the worst place to be was on the end. That was where the most force was applied. Think of a cracking whip. The whip cracks because the end is breaking the sound barrier. For surf torture, the end person got whipped around because of the reaction of the other candidates.

If you're a practically skilled applier of surf torture, you put the "problem" candidates at the end, or whip position, to push them to quit. If you really want an extreme crack, you position the whole line knowing which side the waves will hit first. Imagine the wave at a sporting event, but as the wave travels around the stadium, it gets faster and more intense.

Crashing waves, stinging eyes, and pockets full of sand. The human protest chain against the mighty ocean would never win. This was what you learned. It was futile to resist it, yet once you got in the rhythm and worked as a team, you could take wave after wave and bounce back for more. Even the whip got used to it.

The ocean did not care if you were rich, poor, Black, white, short, tall, male, or female. There had been crashing waves on the beach for millions of years; it would keep crashing wave after wave until the end of time. It was humble and scary to feel the power of the ocean and know that the only way to survive was to link arms, not fight it, and ebb and flow with the power of the ocean.

Even though surf torture was a team sport, each individual had to pull their own weight. The ones that didn't usually quit, because the rest of the team knew they couldn't get out of their own private pity party to do their part.

Although Kokoro was a team event, it was much more about an individual's ability to step outside their own pain and suffering to complete the mission. It was this self-sacrifice in the face of pain and fatigue that changed forever how I looked at the challenges life threw at me.

From: *Jarie Bolander*
Date: *January 31, 2016 at 11:31 p.m.*
Subject: *Jane on Fire!*
To: *janes-care-circle* ▼

An update from Team Jane Forward Operating Base (FOB) Geary is long overdue. The last almost week has been particularly busy and stressful. The bad part of chemo starts after the treatment is completed.

Fevers, mood swings, rashes all over your body, sores in your mouth/esophagus/stomach, trouble eating and sleeping. To top it all off is the neutropenia (which is when someone has very few white blood cells, basically no immune system), which is the reason there is a nicely printed sign on the door that reads: "At Patient's Request, All Who Enter Must Wear a Mask."

Things escalated when the low-grade fevers began. The protocol is that when a chemo patient is neutropenic, they must get blood cultures drawn, and that means more poking at two different sites for each blood draw. Nurses were starting to get scared to draw blood from Jane because if they weren't that experienced, they would poke her in the wrong place, and nothing would come out. The big guns, the seasoned nurses, were brought in. The fevers occurred three days in a row, which meant lots and lots of pricking. Jane was starting to feel like a human pin cushion.

For all the many chemo symptoms, doctors have all sorts of cocktails to provide relief. The best one, magic mouthwash, helps Jane eat. It's actually formulated in the pharmacy, made to order, so to speak, and she looks forward to it before each and every meal. It's got lidocaine, which is the shot you get that numbs you when you get a procedure done, along with a cocktail of many other things that take a PharmD to pronounce. And you thought pharmacists only counted pills.

Finally, four days later, she had 36 hours without a fever, and they were able to put in a new PICC line. Hallelujah! Praise the Lord and pass the gluten-free vanilla pudding.

This was not a fun update to write, but it's the truth about cancer and chemo and Jane's experience. The good thing is Jane is mentally strong and is not knocked down by all of this. She loves binge-watching TV, and there are lots of great shows and movies on cable.

In fact, she had a perfect Jane moment with the doctors. As most of you know, the first bone marrow aspirate got "lost" at the lab, and Jane had to get another one so they could do the cytogenesis to determine Jane's risk factor. Thankfully, she is low/intermediate risk, which means no bone marrow transplant. Yippee! But that's not the fun part.

The fun part was when the two doctors were trying to explain all of this to her during rounds. Apparently, in doctor school, they don't teach you how to get your story straight or maybe talk to each other or maybe just apologize when you have dug yourself into a rat hole so deep that the only thing you can say is "Maybe you should talk to a social worker." Oh no, you didn't.

That comment set Jane off, and I quote, "I don't need a social worker. I have plenty of friends and family to talk to. I want to know why I'm getting a different story than Dr. Lee told me. Also, I want to know for sure. No 'it looks like' or 'preliminary results show.' I want concrete results." The docs never had a chance against a hormone-hopped-up Jane with all the facts at her disposal. Johnny Cochran got nothing on Jane. She was on fire.

One piece of advice Jane got from a lymphoma patient was that even though people are caring for you, they don't really care about you. You always have to advocate for yourself, even if you think you're being a bitch.

Thanks to everyone that has been bringing food. It's all been wonderful. Jane liked them all. That's the honest truth since she still has her taste buds.

Much love,
Team Jane
Operation: DYN-O-MITE
One Team. One Fight. One Jane.

CHAPTER 9

Jane on Fire!

I caught a nasty cold a week before Jane's final chemo treatment and could barely get out of bed. The sinus-pressure-headache-running-nose-fog made it hard to focus on anything, even after the heroic dose of DayQuil I'd use to start my morning. I should have anticipated getting sick after sleeping in a hospital full of sick people, sleep deprivation, and a type-2-diabetes-inducing diet of old-fashioned donuts and blueberry scones. What gutted me was that I had to leave Jane alone and burden her parents with picking up the slack, although they were happy to do so.

We had all been through a lot in the prior month and a half—diagnosis, IVF, chemo. I had gained what felt like ten pounds as a result of devouring whatever was lying around and eating at odd times of the day and night. I was taking catnaps to fight sleep deprivation and drinking double shots of espresso to focus on work and making sure I had an ample supply of 3:1 CBD vape cartridges to take the edge off. But that edge was getting sharper and sharper.

By day three of my required sick leave away from Jane, her chemo symptoms and side effects had emerged and were getting worse. Jane woke me up late one night with a string of texts:

i need u to be the rock right now
even if i seem strong
and i need u to figure out how to do that
without my help
where the hell are you?
why r u not responding to me?
r u drinking again?
I'm CALLING FOR YOUR HELP
and you ARE IGNORING ME
that is NOT OKAY
i look forward all day to have u come back hm

I had to read her texts three times because the NyQuil I had taken put a Vaseline sheen over everything I read. Why was she doing this to me right now? It was 10 p.m. and I was sick and exactly where I didn't want to be—away from her. Deep breath. *Stay calm.* I was so exhausted and medicated that the failure lump had yet to form.

Me: I look forward to that too

She texted back immediately.

Jane: even tho i know u really don't even want to be here
Jane: it never feels like u really do
Me: I want to be there. I have a lot to do.
Jane: sorry i know ur feeling a lot of pressure
Jane: I'm just really sad that u won't be here tonight
Jane: but i know u can't control being sick

At least she gave me that. I willed myself to focus on something sweet and meaningful to say.

Me: So am I. It breaks my heart every time I see you suffer. I die a little inside every time.
Jane: yeah but i want u to be strong for me
Jane: rather than die a little
Jane: U should b here taking care of me!!
Me: I know. I wish I was.
Jane: These last few days have been the worst yet
Jane: My whole body had a rash
Jane: Hair almost gone

Strong for her! I wanted to scream. Couldn't she see that I was trying? Why did she think I was sick? I was busting my ass to keep it together, and all she could do was criticize me for not being strong enough. *Do you know how many other people would have bailed on you?* I wanted to write back. *Give me a break!* But I contained my emerging rage and wrote the supportive thing I knew she needed me to say.

Me: Oh no. I'm sorry you have to deal with that alone. Really, shit.
Me: I should be there. I feel bad about that.
Jane: I get gnarly shivers
Jane: Yeah that's when u keep saying u miss me or u want to hear my voice, i feel that is annoying. Cuz I want u to bolster me up now
Me: Oh man. That sounds awful.
Jane: Instead of you needing me
Me: I did not mean it that way.
Jane: It comes across that way . . . like very needy
Jane: Instead I'd rather u keep asking me questions about the hell I endured and listen and take it in

Actually, she was right there. I was feeling needy—desperately so. Needy for someone to appreciate me and what I was doing. No one asked about me—ever. They only asked about Jane. Jane's illness had taken over my entire life. The only conversations I ever had with anyone were about Jane: *How's Jane? When will Jane be done with chemo? When can I visit?* And my favorite: *Let me know if I can do anything.*

What can you do? How about stop putting the burden on me to tell you what to do? DO SOMETHING already. Geez. What a nightmare!

I willed myself to calm down. Another sequence of deep breaths. None of my reactions to this would help Jane right now. I needed to acknowledge what she was going through, bring this to an end, and go to bed.

> **Me:** I'm sorry you hear that. It's not needy. I just like spending time with you. Of course, I want to take care of you and bolster you up.
> **Me:** Will do.
> **Jane:** Yeah but I don't have the capacity to spend time w anyone. You should b the one to be here to support me and watch me go thru all the pokes
> **Jane:** They had to do another blood culture last night and the nurse could barely get blood out
> **Jane:** All the stuff spilled to the ground
> **Me:** Fuck. That's awful. Getting pricked is no fun at all.
> **Jane:** I'm at a really low pt now
> **Jane:** i think i just really miss you and our personal time together
> and I'm scared that you think i look like a gremlin
> **Me:** I miss our time together as well.
> **Me:** You are not a gremlin. You are GI Jane. I can't wait to shave your head :-)

Putting the phone down on my nightstand, I thought about how Jane and I had always relied on texts to share our feelings. Early in our relationship, it was a lifeline, a love line, a way to share feelings and yet still be protected from them. For me, texting was easier because I could take a few moments to formulate my thoughts before communicating. Since I'd gotten sick, the more open, vulnerable kind of texts had become the norm. I'd meant it when I said I felt horrible that I couldn't be there with her as she struggled. Now I knew that the best I could do was FaceTime her, since this was the only night one of her parents could not spend the night with her. I picked the phone back up and opened the app. She answered on the first ring.

There was Jane's bloated face and tearful eyes, and I took her in, trying not to reveal how my heart was sinking. I could see how much she was suffering. My anger over being woken up and the snarky text messages melted away as I gained my composure to do what I could to help her.

"Babe. It will be okay. You're safe. Nothing is going to happen to you," I said.

"I don't care. I'm freaking out. You're not here. No one is here." Jane was sobbing as she tried to hold the phone and talk to me. "No one cares. These nurses all suck. No one is giving me a straight answer."

My heart was breaking. What was I supposed to say? "Look, I know this is hard and it's scary. I wish I could be there. I really do. You know that, right?"

"Yes. Why did you have to get sick? You need to take better care of yourself. No more Muni." As Jane's tears subsided, she was getting angry at the universe. "So many butts and balls on Muni. Everyone coughs. You can't take Muni. You also have to wear a mask outside."

She had come around to my way of thinking about Lyft because it cost so much money, but she couldn't control how I got around—and I didn't point out the obvious, which was that I was sick because of the hospital, or because of stress, or a combination of both.

Still, I preferred the anger to the tears.

"Yeah. You're right. I'll just work more from the hospital room. That way I won't get sick." I wasn't convinced this was logical but hoped it would make her happy.

"Really? But what about Alena and Matt?" Alena and Matt helped out at the office twice a week, and most of my adventures outside the hospital were about managing them. I also liked having an excuse to leave to self-medicate on espresso and scones.

"They can work from home, or we'll figure something out. Don't worry. Things will get better."

She seemed to calm down a bit and blew her nose.

"Are you feeling better?" Jane refocused on my image on her phone. She was legally blind without her glasses and usually wore contacts, but that was ill-advised given the state of her immune system.

"Yeah. Still have a runny nose, but I'm feeling much better." That was only a half-truth. My head was throbbing, and it was hard to sleep, even in my own bed. NyQuil helped but made me foggy the next day. I was relying on DayQuil to pull me out of the fog when I woke up, along with plenty of espresso.

"Don't come back until you're fully well. I can't afford to get sick. They think I might have an infection now. It's awful. The fever, shivering, hallucinations, and all the blood draws. I can't get any sleep." Her voice was hoarse, and she started to cry again. "I want to go home. I can't do this anymore." Her lips drew into a pout as her eyes scrunched tight to try to hold back the flowing tears that were streaming down her face.

I cried with her—I couldn't help it.

"I know it's hard, but you're tough."

I wanted to hold her hand and tell her it was going to be okay. This was the first time I'd felt the whole experience as a form of torture for both of us.

"It's too much. It's too much."

"Hey, babe," I said, trying to bring her back to me. "Listen to me." Jane looked up from the phone screen with bloodshot, tearful eyes. "I know this is hard. It fucking sucks. Just try not to think about it. Take it a minute at a time. Breathe into it. Let's take some deep breaths together. Breathe in. Breathe out."

We took deep breaths together.

"Do you feel a little better now?" I smiled and tried to put on my best "things will be fine" face.

"A little bit. I'm still pissed that they don't know what's going on with me. I'm seeing shit—like people, animals, blobs of light—and no doctor can tell me what's going on. I'm so angry with them."

Anger is good, I thought. *Get mad at it so we can get through it.* I'd been screaming at leukemia ever since we found out.

"They're doing the best they can." This time I used my calm, late-night DJ voice, but she wasn't convinced.

"*Results.* That's what matters. I want *concrete results*," she emphasized.

"I'll call Cathy tomorrow and ask what's going on." Cathy was the nurse coordinating Jane's care.

She then finally told me what had sparked her anger. The doctors had stopped by that afternoon to give her what they considered good news. They had figured out that they had lost her sample for DNA analysis. But we already knew that. Their obvious attempt to placate her made her furious. "They are all useless. If I did this with clients, I'd get fired. What's so hard about this?"

"I have no idea." I needed some sleep, so I changed the subject. "Did they give you the Ativan yet?"

"Not yet." Jane rang the nurse call button, and within a minute a nurse was handing her a little cup of pills. That cheered her up.

"I need to get going. Do you feel a little better?" I tried to hold back my tears for one more minute.

"Yeah. A little. I miss you. Get better soon. No Muni."

"Got it. Love you."

I must have cried for at least fifteen minutes after I put down the phone and before eating two squares of Kiva chocolate edibles chased with a couple of Tagamets on top of the NyQuil. I hoped all that would calm me down enough to sleep and stave off the heartburn that had been plaguing me every morning when I woke up.

My emotions ran the gamut from sadness and guilt to anger and overwhelm. It seemed the only things within my control were daily doses of cannabis, Tagamet, espresso, scones, and an occasional glass of single malt. I was eating like shit. Emily was making me delicious, healthy food, but I followed every meal with a pint of Ben & Jerry's AmeriCone Dream and half a bag of Haribo Goldbears from City Center Target.

I suppose I was eating my guilt. I felt better when I was away from the hospital, especially sleeping in my own bed. At the hospital, all I did was catch her up on JSY, endure Jane's hour-long bedtime ritual, and then escape to my secret staircase to vape the day away.

Jane was falling deeper into her moods, often stir-crazy from confinement, and lashing out. I couldn't blame her for that, but it was hard to believe how much had changed in little more than a month.

I missed our old life. I missed my wife.

CHAPTER 10

Fear and Loathing

A couple of days after our tearful FaceTime chat, Jane started to feel better. No one ever explained what had made her so sick. I was glad it was behind us and that I felt well enough to be with her.

I easily fell back into the monotonous hospital routine—breakfast, lunch, dinner, blood draws, and bedding changes on a regular schedule, which we actually looked forward to because it marked the passing of another day. The feeling was similar to running a marathon when what keeps you going is getting to the next water stop, and the next, and the next. *Keep going*, you tell yourself, *it will be over soon*. But, of course, with cancer you wake up the next day and you're Bill Murray in *Groundhog Day*—same faces, same places, same cornbread chicken.

The grind of boredom made it hard to focus, but we gradually got used to it. I sometimes worked from the hospital room, but the Internet was so slow that it was impossible to get much done. We knew all the chemo nurses, learned to anticipate their shift changes, and figured out what the CBC numbers meant. My favorite escape (besides the secret stairs)

60

was the Panera up the street from the hospital, which provided two things that made me happy: double espressos and orange-glazed scones. Sometimes I'd sneak Jane a spinach and bacon egg soufflé, dutifully microwaved to kill any possible contamination. A feast.

Becoming the caregiver for your spouse was what the "in sickness" part meant in marriage vows. Of course, there are variable degrees of "in sickness," and most couples might switch between partner and caregiver for maybe a day or two, two or three times a year. With an illness like leukemia, the switch was abrupt and total—not unlike what it must feel like when a newborn comes into your life. The caregiving was something that you could get used to since if you honored your vows, you had no choice. The tricky part was dealing with other people, especially random people.

I didn't blame people for not knowing what to say or focusing just on the sick person. I did blame them for standard responses like, "Things always happen for a reason," or "It's God's will." So many platitudes take no account of the realities someone in crisis is going through. But I'm afraid I've used similar phrases myself to avoid real, gut-wrenching conversations. We all do.

How do you talk to someone who is watching their spouse or partner battle a life-threatening disease? How do you comfort someone whose child, sibling, or parent died? I still don't have all the answers. For me, this experience was so painful that I hoped I would wake up one day to find it was a bad dream. I fantasized about the sun rising on the day Jane was cancer-free. In the evening we could go out to a real restaurant for a romantic dinner. The night I could touch my wife again or kiss her without fear that I would make her sicker.

I was becoming isolated and lonely, as if I were watching a movie about my life, not living it. It was hard to cope with the loneliness and the loss of intimacy. That's why I would fill the void with caffeine, sugar, and CBD. It gave me the needed hit of dopamine that I couldn't get anywhere else. I also figured out how to handle the requests for help. I'd say, "I'll get back to you," and never do so.

AFTER A LITTLE OVER FOUR WEEKS, IT was finally time to go home from the hospital. We almost didn't believe it. We had survived the first round of chemo. By a minor miracle, we hadn't killed each other or the staff.

Chemo causes something called "chemo brain," which makes people forgetful and irritable. Mix that with feeling like shit because you can't sleep and have mouth sores, a stomach lining that's half gone, and the hot flashes of premenopause, and you can see why cancer patients are offered Ativan for anxiety. The world felt like it was slowing down, making ordinary frustrations hard to handle. Patients are often on a fistful of drugs to resolve some of these problematic side effects of treatment. Jane was on antifungal, antibacterial, and antiviral meds, along with Tagamet to keep her heartburn at bay. I couldn't imagine what she would be like without them.

"When can we go? I'm sick of being here. Go ask them again!" She was impatient and pacing around the room in her favorite pair of sweatpants, a white tank top, matching zip-up hoodie, and her Nike workout shoes.

"I asked them ten minutes ago. They're waiting for the discharge paperwork." I was checking email, trying to keep up with all the JSY work.

"Go ask again. You have to fight for things. Be my advocate. Stop being so nice. You do this all the time, letting people roll over you." Jane was more irritated than usual.

"That's not true. How many times do I have to ask?" I raised my voice. Her complaints were getting old. "I want to get out of here too, you know. Do you think I like sleeping here?"

"I want you to keep asking until we actually get out of here. I want to go home." She started to cry. "I want to feel normal, be in a normal bed, eat normal food. *Please.*"

The mood swings were getting worse, and there was nothing to do but comply. I headed into the hallway and made a list in my head: Ativan to calm her down, liquid Benadryl to knock her out. We also needed some chocolate-covered blueberry edibles. Jane loved those, and they always put her in a better mood and helped her appetite.

I could feel her hovering as I stepped toward the doorway, urging me along, so I turned around. Taking her in at that moment was a punch to the gut. She'd changed in just a month. She was thinner but also bloated, mumbling to herself as she paced around. I told myself it was going to be better when we got to Walnut Creek, with more people to help, more familiar surroundings.

I made my way toward the nurses' station. I forced myself to take a deep breath. *Don't take anything personally. Focus on the task at hand. Don't take no for an answer. Be that guy—the dick who always gets his way. The one you hate.*

Before I even opened my mouth, the discharge nurse handed me a stack of papers and a bag of drugs. "You guys are free to go," she said. "Do you need a wheelchair?"

"Um. Sure. I can take this one." I gestured toward a shiny chair nearby.

"Works for me."

I triumphantly returned to our room with the wheelchair, papers, and drugs, in a better mood. "We're all set. We can go now." I was actually smiling.

Jane was not smiling. "It's about time. What took so long?"

"Took so long? I was gone for less than three minutes!" I said. "Let's get going. Let me make sure we have everything. I don't want you to have to come back any time soon."

I double-checked the bag Jane had already triple-checked. I would give anything to never come back here, but I knew that was wishful thinking.

ONCE WE WERE BACK IN A REAL HOUSE with real food, Jane's mood immediately got better. We settled in with her parents for the second stage of the recovery from chemo.

Tim and Emily lived in a single-story ranch home with a perfectly white carpet and a living room that we were only allowed to glance at in passing because it was reserved for entertaining guests, not family. The house was on a quiet tree-lined street close to Mount Diablo. It was spacious and comfortable enough for all of us, with a big backyard, garden, and three-car garage, a third of which was still storing our wedding presents. The grand plan of moving out of our one-bedroom apartment and into a house was a distant memory.

Jane had already started losing her hair at the hospital, but it got worse during our first week at her parents' house. It came out in odd clumps, leaving patches that looked like a patched backyard lawn where dogs relieved themselves. She could hide it under a beanie, but the wisps of hair were so unruly that they'd dance in the breeze when we opened the back door. We realized we had to do something, and she agreed that I could give her a buzz cut like I had promised to do a few weeks before. Just like Demi Moore in *G.I. Jane.*

"Sit in the chair." I motioned for her to sit down on a chair I had positioned in the center of the kitchen. I already had a towel draped over my arm like a real barber.

"I don't know. I kinda like the curls on the end. Looks cute under the hat," she said as she struck a Madonna-type Vogue pose, her hands framing her face.

"C'mon. It looks weird. It won't take too long."

I felt like Hunter S. Thompson buzzing Johnny Depp's hair

to play him in *Fear and Loathing in Las Vegas*, sans the cigarette holder, Crown Royal, and .357 Magnum—all of which I was thinking of (especially the Crown Royal) as I started on Jane's hair.

"Make sure not to nick my head."

"I have the guard on. Don't worry. I'll be careful."

It turns out there is something deeply satisfying about buzzing your wife's head. Maybe it's the primate in us wanting to groom each other. When it was done, I gave Jane a mirror to look at it.

"I look like a Shaolin monk," she said as she stared at her reflection.

"Ha. Your head is so round. Like an egg." I snickered a little. It was true; her head was perfectly round. With her glasses and bald head, she looked a little like a young David Carradine in *Kung Fu.*

Jane's eyes started to well up. "Looks like you got a rotten egg." To my surprise, she was really crying. Her glasses fogged up, and her lower lip quivered. "I'm a rotten egg. I'm sorry, babe. You should leave me." She took off her glasses to wipe her eyes.

I gave her a hug and tried to hold back my own tears. She hadn't seemed this fragile at the hospital.

I hadn't given any real thought to what the loss of hair would mean to Jane. She'd had beautiful long black hair and was always so proud of it. Her hair was one of the things I'd noticed first when I met her. Now she was bald and didn't look the same, but she was still my Jane.

"Hey! No, I didn't get a rotten egg," I told her. "Don't say that. It's going to be fine."

She stopped crying and put her glasses back on. "I hope so. I hope the chemo got the cancer. I don't know if I could go through all that again. It was torture, babe. I mean real torture. Chemo sucks."

Her mood had shifted again, this time from sad to mad. I didn't know if I'd ever get used to these mood shifts.

We tried to cope one day at a time, but cancer is a beast that plays with your mind. Sometimes I actually thought I had given Jane leukemia because she was diagnosed when we were trying to get pregnant. I knew that was silly, with no scientific basis, but I wanted an answer and there were none.

Everything about the leukemia was still, after all those weeks, unknown, like how she got it and if chemo would cure her. The doctors and nurses were not hiding anything from us; they were frustrated by the unknowns too. They had all been kind, especially the cancer nurses. Cancer nurses are saints, putting up with so many mood swings and complications in all their patients. I was in awe and hopeful that what Jane had endured would cure her leukemia.

CHAPTER 11

The Joys and Sorrows
of Recovery

Jane's recovery was a perpetual rickety rocket ride on one of those old-fashioned wood and cable roller coasters like the Giant Dipper on the Santa Cruz Beach Boardwalk. No matter how many times I thought I had it figured out, on the next climb to the apex the ride was different. I tried to anticipate the twists and turns, but somehow I always timed them wrong or made the mistake of assuming I had figured it out.

After about six weeks, I was finally getting the hang of JSY, but it was harder to get the hang of Jane. I often got long text threads like this:

> **Jane:** do u wonder how i do in the day? or ur just
> focused on your own stuff?
> **Jane:** it just still feels like u abandon me mostly, and
> use the work as an excuse and then yell at me when i
> say something about it. It's really unfair
> **Me:** I do wonder and I am not just focused on my own
> stuff. I'm sorry that you feel it's unfair.

Jane: my own friends reach out more than u and don't give me work as an excuse
Me: That makes me feel sad that you would say that.
Jane: if u don't want to ride thru this hard time with me, there is no pt in being married
Me: That's a ridiculous statement. I'm a ride or die kinda guy. My apologies for not reaching out sooner.
Jane: it seems more like a disappearing into work kinda guy
Me: Not at all.
Jane: I'm not here in this world to do the monkey dance for u . . . and make u smile
Me: Okay. I will do more monkey dances and check in more often. My bad. I'm sorry about that.

She was right. I did want to disappear sometimes, especially if she was in the hospital. I didn't mind sleeping at her parents' house, where we were currently staying, since it was easy to spread out. The only downside was its farther distance from our office in San Francisco. I don't like conflict, and the stress and strain of everything was taking its toll on me. I wanted our old life back, but I knew that might never happen. This feeling of being a zero in terms of having the energy and power to fix things for Jane always made the failure lump show up in my throat again, especially when she would text me something like this:

It's odd you don't think i need you
i can hardly see, i feel shivery all the time, no one
knows what the fuck is wrong w me
I'm just stuck here, at home . . . feeling like ass
well i don't have shit to give right now

need to feel the confidence on your own and not have
to get it from others
u want the praise of randoms all the time
thats why u kiss up to randoms
wasting your breath and energy on those people

What stung most was that she was telling the truth. I did want praise from others. I wanted to fill the void of never being good enough, which I knew came from my relationship with my dad. It's one of those things that always drove me to seek praise from others by doing something as opposed to being worthy of affection and praise for being me. But I needed her praise too, and I wanted to listen like she needed me to listen. I wanted to make her happy and do some of the loving and sweet things she did for me, like on my forty-first birthday.

Jane had planned a surprise party for me that year, complete with a fake invitation to a completely different event to throw me off the scent. This was the first time in my life that anyone had done something so special for me. Her smile as we walked into a bar filled with my friends and family said *I did this for you because I love you so much.* My heart felt like it might explode out of my chest. And I felt special just for being me.

Would we ever be able to do those things again? Would I ever be able to do something like that for Jane?

But then I'd get a text that made me want to run away from Jane—or more precisely, from my failure to solve this leukemia problem. I was trying my best, but it was never good enough or fast enough or romantic enough. I couldn't talk to anyone about these feelings. They say it's lonely at the top—well, it was even lonelier in the trench fighting for any scrap of normalcy, intimacy, and sanity when I was a caregiver for my spouse with a terminal illness.

To see how bad Jane was feeling broke open my heart in such a way that my failure lump oftentimes escaped unencumbered. The worst part was that I couldn't do anything to help except try my best to be supportive. I sometimes failed in critical moments because that kind of support was something I hadn't learned from my family growing up. I often had to have some prodding before I noticed people around me in need. It was easy for me to escape into my head, with the proverbial thousand-yard stare of a Vietnam bush marine trying to survive each minute in a jungle that was trying to kill him.

The good news was that Jane always told me what she needed, and I got better at listening. And she got better at giving me a break about my shortcomings and enlightening me on how to be a better person, husband, and caregiver.

Me: How are you feeling? Did you get some rest? I'll be leaving here at 4:26 with your mom.
Jane: i watched a movie with my dad . . .
Jane: but i still feel uneasy . . . body temperature all off, eyes can't see
Jane: it makes me feel sad . . .
Me: That would make me feel sad as well. How about we go for a drive when I get home? Get you out of the house.
Jane: well it'd be nice to walk . . .
Jane: the cancer people have no answers
Jane: am i supposed to take this long to recover
Jane: they don't know shit
Me: Okay. Let's do that. We can drive somewhere different to walk. Maybe downtown and window shop
Jane: do u think i did something bad to get cancer
Me: Not at all. You did nothing bad. Sometimes things just happen. They don't even know what causes leukemia

Jane: i feel like i see all these people online with these new babies, and on the other hand, we are dealing with cancer
Jane: like was i evil or something
Me: You were not evil. You are an awesome person and unfortunately you got cancer. This sometimes happens to even good people. The good news is that you will overcome and be stronger
Jane: thanks for being such a wonderful hubby!
Me: Ah. On the way home. Love you
Jane: Ok. I love you babe!

Whew. We were back to somewhat of a normal interaction. But the rickety rocket zero-to-hero roller-coaster ride would take off again soon, and the ride was going to get worse. The world was random and chaotic, and the only easy day was yesterday.

JANE HAD A STANDING ORDER FOR A CBC twice a week to monitor her immune system's recovery and to make sure she didn't need any platelets or red blood cells.

They took out the PICC line before we left the hospital to go back to Walnut Creek. She'd have to be tested with normal pricks at the local Walnut Creek Kaiser lab. Usually, it took two to three weeks for someone's immune system to recover and start producing all the cells needed to survive. After looking at lab results for weeks, I got pretty good at interpreting what they meant. I began keeping track of the results in a Google Sheet so I could watch the trends.

Along with the levels of white and red blood cells and platelets, a "percent blasts metric" is an important sign of what's going on in the bone marrow. Blasts are immature blood cells that differentiate into white cells, red cells, or platelets, among other things. Blasts in your peripheral blood (what circulates through your body) could be an early sign of things not going right. It was this blast level and her low red blood cell and platelet levels that had led to her diagnosis in the ER. Most of us have few or no blasts in our peripheral blood—way less than 1 percent of all our cells. But if you have leukemia, your blast count goes up to over 10 percent. The complicating factor in all the measurements was that the CBC machine can sometimes misclassify blasts if they are "amorphous," which means lacking shape, or already dead cells.

Amorphous blasts almost always trick the machine into thinking the patient has more than they really do. After chemo, amorphous blasts become even more pronounced because the patient's bone marrow releases all the dead cells that the chemo killed. It's kind of like a sunburn that starts to peel, when a lot of dead skin falls off so that new skin can come to the surface.

Despite my love of spreadsheets and numbers, I quickly realized that in certain circumstances, ignorance made life easier. When the three days of blood tests came back showing increasing white blood cell counts (good) *and* increasing blasts (bad), Jane started to freak out.

"Oh no. The cancer's back. Look at the blasts. Oh no." Jane was sitting on her parents' couch, looking at her laptop. The latest blood test showed 15 percent blasts, up from 8 percent in the previous test.

"Hold on. We should talk to Dr. Lee about this. Remember, he said the only way to really tell would be to do another biopsy." My mind was racing to try to calm her down. We were back on the roller coaster, slowly climbing toward the apex of "I'm going to die."

"Oh no. Oh no. Shit. This is bad. I can't believe I have to go through all that again. I don't want to do it." The tears started. Tim, Emily, Eric, and I all looked at Jane's laptop trying to find some good news, but there was none.

"Look, we need to call Dr. Lee and have them do the biopsy. Then we'll know for sure. Let's not freak out yet." That's what I said, but my thoughts were much different. That failure lump was lodged deep in my throat, and the acid in my stomach was basically the stuff the Alien spit at Ripley, rapidly burning through the entire ship, deck after deck, with no way to stop it.

"This is bad." Jane had stopped crying and had her face in her hands. She mumbled, "Fuck. Fuck. Fuck," to herself quietly. The four of us stared at each other, not knowing what to say or do. Finally, Jane lifted her head and said, "I'm going to eat some edibles and go to sleep," before walking to her room.

The family sat motionless for a while. Then Emily started to make dinner, Eric and Tim went outside to the garden, and I added the results to my Google spreadsheet.

The next day we called Dr. Lee, and his office set up an appointment for the biopsy. A couple of days later, we got the news: The leukemia was back, and Dr. Lee said Jane needed a bone marrow transplant (BMT). That would be the best shot at curing her. Until a donor could be found, Jane would have to do a chemo cycle every four to six weeks to keep the leukemia at bay.

My heart sank. More chemo. More hospitals. More feeling like shit. This was going to be harder than any of us had imagined.

CHAPTER 12

Reality Bites

WHEN JANE GOT SICK, THE LAST THING on my mind was to ask for help. In fact, I had a hard time even figuring out how to ask for help. It's this attitude that had been the lens through which I lived my life and tried to escape my own private pity party that was a Cineplex mix of *Dazed and Confused*, *The Breakfast Club*, and *Say Anything*, trying to stave off *Reality Bites*. But this was where we were headed.

My generation, Generation X, was the first generation to be latchkey kids, with both parents working, single mothers struggling to make ends meet, and the last to get their drivers' permits in high school under the watchful eyes of chain-smoking teachers who would crack the window to light up a Camel to calm their nerves.

Our parents are a mix of Lost Generation and Early Boomers who were trying to find themselves and consume as much of the cocaine-fueled go-go '80s as possible. My dad was a farm boy from Parsons, Kansas, who packed up his '55 Chevy that ate as much oil as gas for the trek to the Golden State via Route 66. He made it to Barstow before hitchhiking his way to Oakland. My mom was an immigrant from World War II–devastated Holland via colonial Aruba, where she learned how to be a lady at private school so she could start her career as a hairdresser and finish it as a drug store clerk.

My siblings and I were largely left to raise ourselves on reruns of *Gilligan's Island*, *Hogan's Heroes*, *Green Acres*, and *The Beverly Hillbillies* while sustaining ourselves on Hot Pockets, Pop-Tarts, and Cap'n Crunch.

What little money we had was scraped together by paper routes, fast-food jobs, and the rare allowance after the age of ten. With our savings, my friends and I bought an Atari 2600 so we could stay up all night playing *Space Invaders*, *Donkey Kong*, and *Asteroids* with our friends at overnight sleepovers where we stayed up all night eating Pop Rocks chased with Pepsi.

Serial killers and abductions were our "mass shootings," yet we still roamed our neighborhoods, building bike ramps out of wood we stole from construction sites, smoking shake pot out of soda can pipes, and playing doorbell ditch until the streetlights told us it was time for our Swanson's Hungry-Man turkey TV dinner with mashed potatoes, gravy, and my favorite—apple-cranberry cake cobbler. The trick for perfect cobbler was to carefully peel the aluminum foil around it so it could get nice and crispy, something we were proud that we could do on our own.

For us, the cavalry was never going to come. We had to figure it out. We were ride or die with each other and didn't even know it.

If we made it to college, it was either community college or a public state university, which was still affordable with a modest student loan.

This is all to say that my family of origin was not emotionally supportive, yet we'd be happy to help you do some tasks as long as it did not involve money.

I can hardly remember praise for a job well done except when I graduated from college. Usually, the cards in my family had Hallmark quotes with only "Love, Mom and Dad" in my mom's handwriting. In my graduation card, my dad wrote: "I'm proud of you for getting your college degree. Dad."

I remember only one time where the overstep of authority pissed my dad off so much that he called the Hayward Police to defend my honor. It was the latter half of November 1988 and the news had been filled with the disappearance of Michaela Garecht, a nine-year-old girl who'd vanished a couple of blocks from her home in Hayward that same month. A concerned citizen had called and said they saw someone who they believed to be the kidnapper parking in front of Carlmont High School. That someone was me.

To be fair, I did look like the artist's sketch of a tall, thin white guy with a mullet and pockmarked face. My car, a burnt-gold Bondo-and primer-riddled 1969 Pontiac Tempest, also matched the description of the kidnapper's car. But what set my dad off was that they pulled me out of class and searched my car without calling him or being more discrete. It was the only time I'd ever heard him swear over the phone.

From the moment Jane got sick, I knew I'd resist asking for help from my family. That wasn't the type of people we were. I'd keep inside my private pity party and not rely on anyone for anything. That was in my comfort zone, though probably not the healthiest solution for anyone. Yet Jane's family was much different. They wanted to help, and I'd have to learn to embrace and appreciate help from family and friends even though deep in my gut it made my failure lump surge to the back of my throat. The soloist attitude is hard to shake when it's been that way for the better part of your life.

CHAPTER 13

Family Field Trip to the Farm

JANE HAD TO GO THROUGH SEVERAL rounds of chemo to keep the leukemia at bay until a bone marrow match could be found, which meant we were going to be playing a tricky waiting game and spending more time in the hospital.

Chemotherapy's goal is to kill off cancer cells while not killing the patient. As a patient progresses through rounds of therapy, the cancer cells that remain become more resilient, and this escalates the stakes. The more resilient the cancer, the stronger the chemo they need, which creates more resilient cancer cells, and so on . . . At some point in this escalation, if the cancer hasn't killed them, the side effects of chemo will.

Kaiser outsources its bone marrow transplants (BMTs) to Stanford, known to alumni as "the Farm." BMT was covered under our insurance, which was a relief because a lot of the policies we had looked at before picking Kaiser did not fully cover the chemo or did not cover the BMT at all.

I can't imagine what it would have been like to worry about Jane's treatment and at the same time have to worry about how to pay for all she needed to keep her alive. It was a stressful, full-time job to keep up with all the appointments and details. Throwing fears about financing everything on top of that would have been a next level of purgatory with the bottom of the ladder slowly being consumed by flames—and lots of people face that hell every day.

This new treatment option was going to be more intense for Jane and more work for me because we would have to move to Palo Alto. This meant I'd have to commute to San Francisco regularly, where JSY's office was located, which prompted another hard conversation.

"I think we should shut down JSY for a while," I said, being careful with when and how I broached this conversation with Jane. Usually, the best time was in the afternoons, right after her nap. On this particular day, her parents had gone to the market, so we were alone at their house. "We really need to focus on making you better." I had been thinking about the business implications more and more, ever since we'd made the trek to Stanford to get the details on bone marrow transplants.

"No. No. No. I don't want to do that. We need the money." Jane looked up from her laptop. She was feeling better and trying to work, which seemed to take her mind off being sick.

"No, we don't. We have plenty for now, and insurance is taking care of almost everything. I should really be focused on you full-time."

"No. No. No. We can do it. Look at all the work we have, and the new clients. You're doing great. *Please. Please. Please.* We can't just shut down my baby." How could she say I was doing great? I was vaping every night so I could fall asleep. I couldn't clear my mind of all the client requests and the worry about her treatment. Something had to give.

"Babe, the business will be there when you're better. Besides, I suck at it. I have no idea what I'm doing." I had been running JSY for over six months, and it was agony. I hated it and thought the time in Palo Alto would be perfect for taking a break. I would have given anything to go back to writing code, where perfection was just a recompile away.

"I know. It's hard. That's why PR is one of the most stressful jobs out there." Jane put an arm around me. "You're doing great, and the clients love you. You understand all the technology stuff, and you can write!" She started to pat my back, and I felt like a hero again, but I wasn't going to give up the argument so quickly.

"What about when we're at Stanford? I don't want to commute to the city daily to manage the staff. We need to get rid of them. It's ridiculous that I have to commute to manage them. It's a waste of time!" I was starting a rant—my usual way of dealing with shit that was out of my control. "We need to simplify, and that starts with not having to commute."

"Okay. Okay. We can sort that out. But I need to keep JSY. We need something to do, and I like it. It keeps my mind off the cancer."

"It stresses us both out," I argued. "You're always panicked about a client firing us or getting them coverage or whatever. I can't handle all this. It's too much." I was almost yelling. The lump of failure was trying to creep into my throat, but I was punching that demon down. This time my anger and adrenaline were going to win. Finally, I could share how I really felt. All this work anxiety was over some stupid clients with stupid requests, and their stupid money that we didn't even need.

Jane wasn't going to give in, though. "Everything is going to work out. Trust me. You're doing great. We'll sort out how to handle the staff." She repeated her own arguments, ones that were hard for me to push back on: it was a great distraction, and JSY meant too much to her. She continued to rub my back as I bowed my head and put my face in my hands, exhausted, frustrated, and defeated. My frustration started to wane, and I realized this was why I loved her so much. In the face of unimaginable stress and strain, she could keep it together when I was losing my shit.

I had been thinking nonstop about the cancer coming back and how to cure Jane. It was scary as hell to imagine that we had to find a donor to save her life. The whole donor process was a one-in-a-million-shot-in-the-dark-from-a-mile-away-in-a-hurricane-type nightmare, compounded in part by the fact that Jane was Asian.

The number of Asian and minority donors in the bone marrow registry is a lot lower than the number of Caucasians. Apparently when the bone marrow registry was getting started, they transferred over all the people who donated blood, and those blood donors were mostly white. For a transplant to be successful, the genes have to match as much as possible, or the transplant will not take. Jane also had a rare allele (gene variant) that was hard to match.

A week earlier, we'd contacted the Asian American Donor Program (AADP), which specializes in finding Asian donors. AADP had done several successful drives, and they had saved a couple of dozen people through their efforts.

The doctors told us the odds of finding a non-relative donor were slim to none because even though AADP did a lot of outreach, the number of Asian donors was still small. Our best bet was that Eric, Jane's brother, was either a perfect match or a haplo match (half match). During the same week we connected with AADP, Eric had his test to see what kind of a match he might be. That would take upwards of a month to come back, so we decided to hedge our bets and try and find a donor as well. Either way, the odds of a complete recovery were diminishing. The odds were still above 50 percent if the next round of chemo could get Jane into remission or complete remission 2 (CR2), as the docs called it. But remission was only half the story.

All BMT patients risk getting graft-versus-host disease (GVHD), which is when a person's new immune system attacks their body. Jane was freaked out by the prospect of this because the symptoms were particularly nasty—tight skin, blurry vision, and gastrointestinal bleeding, to name a few.

Statistics are funny things. When you look at the one-, three-, and five-year survival rates for leukemia on the Internet, you find all these studies with low numbers of participants, as well as meta studies (studies of studies) that had all sorts of variables that hardly made any sense. Add to the mix that there are several different types of leukemia, and having to account for how healthy or unhealthy someone was when they got it—and the statistics are pretty much bullshit.

The statistics that gave me the most hope were the ones from the Leukemia & Lymphoma Society because their stats were more about actions you could take to increase the odds of getting better. Those actions included exercising, handling other health issues, meditating, and having a support network. The power of that last one was slowly revealing itself as we ramped up Everlasting Plasma (our new military-style code name for saving Jane) to find a donor. Team Jane began to organize more than ten drives all over the world, and we were starting to get help from some of our more notable friends. I was starting to learn how to ask for help and not feel like a total failure.

As Tim and Emily came back from the store, I was feeling a bit better about being able to handle my two full-time jobs. I felt a little calmer that my concerns had been heard and that Jane knew my thought process. We did not always agree on things, but being heard was an important part of moving on from a difficult situation with a plan, even though it was not optional.

CHAPTER 14

My Kingdom for a Donor

EVER SINCE OUR TRIP TO THE FARM AT Stanford, it was nonstop bone marrow drive after bone marrow drive. The outpouring of help was wonderful and took a huge burden off me. The bone marrow drives took a lot of time to organize, but everyone wanted to help out, including our local elected supervisor and good friend London Breed.

The first time I met London was before Jane and I met at London's fundraiser, when I was the president of the North of Panhandle Neighborhood Association in the Western Addition of San Francisco. I'd been working on the 100th Bay to Breakers "running race," a quintessential San Francisco event. Runners dressed up, got drunk, and created mayhem along the seven-mile route from San Francisco Bay to the break at Ocean Beach. Ground zero for the shenanigans—or rather, where all the drunk people passed out—was the Panhandle in Golden Gate Park, my old neighborhood.

Aside from her role in introducing us, London had married us in her capacity as a government official. Through London, we met lots of other elected officials who offered to help us get the word out and find a donor for Jane.

London set up a press conference and bone marrow drive at San Francisco City Hall in the spring of 2016 to raise awareness not only for Jane but also for all minorities waiting for a donor. Jane couldn't attend because she was in the hospital on her second round of chemo.

As I looked around the conference room, I saw dozens of AADP people who had family members with leukemia or knew someone who had it. All had done the exact same thing we were about to do—get the word out about bone marrow donation. Most were minorities who would quietly nod when I would glance over at them. For the first time, I realized how many others, like us, were struggling daily to keep a loved one alive. I had seen all the videos of other patients pleading for a donor, but seeing their family members standing in the room with me focused my energy not only for Jane but also for all those we might be able to help.

The tragedies in our lives can only be tempered by the knowledge that we are not alone in our fights. I must admit that I felt alone in the fight for Jane more often than not. Most people didn't want to know what was going on beyond asking, "How's Jane?"

And even when I knew someone was genuinely interested, it was too hard to open the floodgates of emotion to share what was happening in my head and heart. I was afraid that I wouldn't have the answers they wanted, or worse yet, that I'd have to admit I had no clue what was going to happen. The failure lump firmly shut off any deep or meaningful conversation unless it was in front of a bunch of randoms, like this press conference, but I was prepared and channeled a San Francisco icon, Harvey Milk, to help me get through it; still, I delivered my speech through tear-filled eyes.

The line I borrowed from Harvey was his most well-known—"I'm here to recruit you!" I struggled to hit the mark but forged ahead: "My name is Jarie Bolander, and I'm here to recruit you to help Jane and many others find a bone marrow donor." I paused for a moment, not because I wanted to be poetic but because the tears were welling in my eyes and I could feel the lump surging from my stomach into my throat.

I was so grateful for the opportunity to share my thoughts on the challenges we faced. Thousands of families were dealing with the harsh realities of cancer like Jane's, and in that room, at that moment, I felt I spoke for them all.

For the first time in months, I didn't feel alone.

CHAPTER 15

Too Much

THE SECOND ROUND OF CHEMO WENT BETTER than the last time. A lot better. It only took Jane four weeks to recover. Better still, she had none of the fevers and hallucinations she'd experienced the first time. And when she was feeling better, she wanted to take on more work before we had to move to Palo Alto to start the BMT in mid-June.

Plans for her client Dontari Poe's football camp for kids, which would happen just before the BMT, were coming together nicely. Jane's excitement was building, knowing that if she continued to recover, she would be able to go to the camp, which would be held in Memphis, Tennessee, at Dontari's old high school, in early June. We had our fingers crossed.

Jane made travel fun and always had some sort of surprise or adventure planned. Once, when we went to Palm Springs for a wedding, she'd booked a private sound bath session at the Integratron, "a fusion of art, science, and magic" in Landers, thirty minutes outside of Palm Springs. Legend has it that aliens visited the site to infuse the well water with healing powers. The "energy" within the perfect dome of the Integratron, which had been constructed without nails, made the sound coming out of the assorted quartz bowls vibrate through your whole body.

Overall, JSY was doing okay. We'd held an event for our client Fam 1st Family Foundation, founded by Marshawn Lynch and Josh Johnson, at Oakland Tech High School with Hugh Jackman. Before he became an actor, Hugh had been a gym teacher. Since he was promoting his new movie, *Eddie the Eagle*, they wanted him and Marshawn to teach some kids about sportsmanship and have Josh throw some passes to them. Jane got to attend, and it seemed to both make her happy and stress her out, but more importantly, she felt hopeful that she could return to work.

We had lost a client in April who had been paying us a nice retainer, but I was actually relieved because it meant I could spend more time with Jane. But she took it hard, even though the departure had nothing to do with the quality of our work. Back home after the Fam 1st event, her concerns over money came out.

"How come you're taking out so much cash?" Jane was looking through our bank account. She had always been the one to pay the bills, but I had taken over when she got sick.

"What do you mean?" I was making our standard dinner of steamed rice and a sautéed bunch of fresh spinach with a couple of lean chicken breasts, lightly salted and sautéed in olive oil. It was a far cry from our usual fare at the latest trendy restaurant pre-leukemia.

"It's right here. Over the last three months, it's like . . ." Jane looked at her computer and, with her finger, counted all the cash withdrawals. "It's like three hundred dollars a month!"

"Yeah. So? I needed the cash for stuff."

"Like what? *Coffee? Lunches?*" Jane's tone was condescending. "We can't afford that."

"What do you mean? We have plenty. What am I supposed to do? Not eat?" I didn't understand why we had to talk about money at that moment. It had been a long day. Jane was in a testy mood. She'd been asking me a ton of questions about JSY and second-guessing some of my decisions.

"No more coffee. It's bad for you and expensive," she blurted out as I was finishing cooking our dinner.

I didn't appreciate her bossiness. "How am I supposed to stay awake during the day? Sleeping at the hospital isn't easy." My double espresso with a scone chaser remained one of the main joys in my life, a little slice of sanity and moment of calm on the roller coaster—a dopamine hit that gave me the smallest of reprieves, and I wasn't going to give it up.

"It's *hard* for you to sleep? I get woken up at all hours. It's miserable. You get to leave. I had to stay there for a month!" She was yelling now. "You have no idea how hard it is!"

"I have a pretty good idea. I was there. Remember?" I was now irate as well.

"Yeah, I remember. You left me for a week. You *hated* being there. In the morning, you'd wake up and couldn't wait to leave. Admit it!" Jane had put down the laptop and was scowling at me.

"I did not *hate* being there. I was sick. Remember?" The cauldron of acid in my stomach started to gurgle and bubble. The lump was forming, and it would be a big one. *Not this again.*

Jane wasn't going to let it go this time. "You wanted to leave me, drink your coffee, take the bus, get sick, and eat out. Easy life for you." Her voice had risen an octave, and her scowl had turned into the kind of stare you'd direct at someone who had just ripped you off. She was in rare form, but so was I.

"Give me a break. I wanted to quit JSY so I could focus on taking care of you. If I didn't have to work, then I wouldn't have to leave. *You* wanted me to work on JSY, remember?" I said as I put a plate of food down in front of her.

She snorted dismissively. "Whatever. You hate that too. Your start-up doesn't even pay you. It never has. I've been supporting us for the last two years." Jane's arms were crossed, her posture erect, and her eyes narrowed as she glared at me.

"That's not fair. We discussed this. If I didn't have the flexibility, I couldn't take care of you and run JSY. It's a lot of work."

"You have it *easy* compared to me. You come and go as you please. You can see friends. All I do is sit here or in the hospital or at my parents'. I'm completely *trapped*." Jane was releasing frustrations that had been brewing for months. She was so angry she stood up without touching her food and went into the bedroom and slammed the door, yelling, "You don't understand!"

"You don't have to slam the door," I said to no one. I was still pissed off that I had to take such abuse over a few cups of coffee and a beef gyro platter at Halal Guys.

A couple of minutes later, Jane came out, all dressed and with her beanie on. She grabbed her purse.

"Where are you going? I made dinner. You can't leave."

"You're not the boss of me!" she yelled as she walked through the front door and slammed it behind her.

"Where are you going?" I said, again to no one. I stood in the middle of our living room feeling utterly alone.

Fuck, I thought. *I'm sick of this bullshit. I can't do anything right in her mind.* My thoughts swirled and spiraled. This was hard on me too. I had lost my life partner and got a moody chemo patient in her place. I couldn't even remember the last time we'd had sex or even held each other. It was all go, go, go—go to this appointment. Make sure she takes this medicine. Update everyone on her progress. It was maddening, and I hated what our lives had become.

After a good ten minutes, I calmed down enough to start to worry. I tried Jane's cell phone and got her voice mail. So I texted her:

Me: Where did you go?
Me: Can you at least tell me where you are?
Me: I'll come get you!!!!

Another stressful ten minutes passed.

Jane: U don't give a shit

Me: That is not true

Jane: I gave u the shared google doc about what to do

Jane: I'm riding u because we r gonna lose a client

Me: That is not true at all

Jane: U never believe me then we lose clients

Me: If we lose them, it's not because we are not doing things. It's because they don't have money.

Me: Where are you?

Jane: That's not up to u to decide

Jane: I don't wanna see u now

Me: Where are you?

Jane: U never listen

Me: Just come home and I'll leave so you can be safe and warm

Jane: I'll die on the side of the road and everyone can move on w their lives

Me: Don't say that.

I searched the apartment for the keys to the Camry. I hoped she hadn't taken the car. It would be harder to find her if she was mobile. Luckily, she hadn't. I got dressed and went down to the car and tried to figure out where she would go. The park? Fillmore Street? Hamlin Mansion? I was trying to text and drive at the same time, and she was letting me have it.

Jane: I want to resolve this client stuff

Me: Don't say that. Where are you? I will come get you.

Jane: I poured my blood sweat and tears and I'm asking u to keep it going

Me: I am trying to keep it going.

Jane: I created the google doc cuz I knew we were on the rocks

Me: Okay. Let's go through the doc and see what more we have to do.

Jane: I already shared it w u and u can review on ur own

Me: Okay. Then I'll make it happen or assign it.

Jane: I hate that u argue w me cuz if I become right then it's too late

Jane: And I know my business. I've had it for 11 yrs

Me: Okay. I'll do more for them and focus more on it.

Jane: And I don't know why u argue w me

Jane: Well it may b too late anyways

Me: I don't like being told what to do.

Jane: Well u have no choice here

Me: You're the boss. I'll do the work.

I started to drive in a serpentine pattern from our apartment on Buchanan down to Fillmore Street, passing the hospital and Ales Unlimited. It was still light out, but twilight was fast approaching. The texting while driving was not working. I'd drive a bit and then pull over to answer. I was starting to freak out too. What if something happened to her? What if she got sick? Her immune system was so weak.

Jane: We have lost 4500/month already

Jane: I even fuckin outlined it for u

Jane: And it allows u to have freedom to go w me to appts

Me: Just come home and we can discuss.

Jane: No I have other shit to deal w and everyone's just giving me more stress

Me: You need to come home so you don't catch a cold. It's important that you do this NOW
Jane: I might as well just die of this disease
Me: DON'T SAY THAT. You need to take care of yourself.
Me: Are you coming home?
Jane: No

Shit. Twilight had arrived, and I had no idea when this text argument was going to be over. I tried to call her, but she wouldn't pick up. I was nearly hyperventilating by this point with frustration and fear. What good would I be if I got into a wreck? I pulled over and texted her.

Me: Where are you?
Me: Babe. Don't do this. I'll leave. You have to come home and be here.
Me: It's important. It's about your health.
Jane: I'm not coming hm unless we resolve this client thing
Jane: And u never dispute me again when I'm speaking to u realistically
Me: Okay. It's resolved. You're right. We need to do more busy work.
Jane: Can u come get me?
Me: Where are you?
Jane: Browser books
Me: I'll be right down.

Browser Books was on the corner of Sacramento and Fillmore, less than five blocks from our apartment. It was one of Jane's favorite places. I should have looked there first, but I was too frantic to think.

As I drove around the corner, I saw her standing outside Browsers. I pulled up and opened the door, and she hopped in.

"Hi. Thanks for picking me up," she said, like it was just another ordinary day.

"Sure. Happy to." I wasn't sure what else to say.

She looked at me, buckled her seat belt, and reached for my hand. "I'm starving. Let's go back home and eat."

"Sure. We can do that."

We drove the short distance in silence, holding hands. When we got back to our apartment, we walked the single flight of stairs to our door, and Jane went into our room, emerging five minutes later in sweats, plopping down on the couch. I reheated dinner.

"Let's rent a movie," she said as I brought our plates to the couch and sat down next to her. "I want to see something funny."

We ate as we watched *Blazing Saddles*, laughing at the jokes and not saying much of anything else.

"I don't mind if you drink coffee. I know you enjoy it," Jane said when we got into bed a couple of hours later.

"I can cut back. It's no big deal," I replied, trying to offer an olive branch.

"Don't. I'm sorry I yelled at you about it. I have no control of my life right now. When I saw all the money being spent, it made me mad," she explained as she grabbed my hand and turned toward me in bed.

"I can tell you when I need money. No big deal. Really," I insisted.

"No. No. You don't need to do that. It's your money too."

"I know, but it's important to you. I'll tell you," I said confidently.

"I know this sucks, babe. I'm not in my right mind most of the time. The chemo makes me crazy even when I'm off it." She moved onto her other side and winced, trying to avoid putting pressure on the spot where she'd had the bone marrow biopsy.

"I get it. I know it's hard on you. It's hard on everyone to see how hard it is on you and that we can't help out much." I was looking up at the ceiling. I hated seeing her in pain.

"I'm helpless and dependent," she confessed. "I have no freedom. That makes me sad and mad at the same time. It's too much to take sometimes. That's why I had to get out of the apartment."

"You should have told me where you were going. I was freaked out and worried. Your immune system is still so weak." I looked into her eyes, hoping to make her understand how afraid I'd been.

"Okay. I won't do it again." Jane rolled toward me again, smiling this time. Before leukemia, Jane would rarely get yelling-match angry at me. Usually, she'd get annoyed with me about some subtle silly thing that I would either forget to do or ask her about. Occasionally, she'd get pissed at me for not asking her about her day. That might get a reaction, but nothing like this.

That would not be the last time Jane and I fought about the "normal" things that all couples fight about. But nothing about our arguments was normal anymore. The intense emotions and vulnerability surrounding Jane's illness fueled the fires and raised the stakes of every word and glance. When one five-block walk suddenly felt like a matter of life or death, I knew things had changed. Who could blame her? This was scary, and she was handling it better than I would.

CHAPTER 16

Southern Hospitality

J ane was technically in remission in June, but all that meant
was that the latest round of chemo had beat down her
leukemia enough so that she had a "normal" amount of red,
white, and platelet cells—normal for a person with leukemia.
The doctors still wanted to do the bone marrow transplant
(BMT) because her blast counts were hovering between 5 and
10 percent, which meant the leukemia was not as active.

When the docs cleared Jane for her trip to Memphis, she
was ecstatic to the point of tears. She put down the phone and
told me in a whisper, "I can *go*." She gave me a big hug. It was
the first time in six months I had seen the smile on her face and
in her eyes that I fell in love with.

We had been working on Dontari's football camp since
January and planned a side trip to Nashville to visit friends
afterward. "I can't wait to eat BBQ, sleep in a posh hotel with
turndown service, and drink yummy cocktails," Jane said as she
packed for the trip. She had been beaming and full of energy
for days to the point where she even wanted to cook dinner.
We were both excited to have an adventure and give the kids

the best football camp the city had ever seen at Dontari's alma mater, Wooddale High School.

Dontari had started playing football in high school, went to the University of Memphis, crushed the NFL Combine, and was a first-round, eleventh overall pick for the Kansas City Chiefs in 2012. At six foot three and 345 pounds, he could run a forty-yard dash in 4.98 seconds, but he hadn't even started playing football until his high school coach saw him in the freshman marching band and dragged him onto the team.

Wooddale was surrounded by the poorest zip codes in Tennessee, with some of the highest child poverty rates in the United States. Every kid in southeastern Memphis looked up to Dontari as a hometown hero, so when he brought a first-class football camp to Wooddale, it was a big deal.

Memphis was perched on a bluff along the slow-moving Mississippi River, and in June the city felt like a blast furnace doused with a bucket of barbecue-scented sticky river water that condensed on every window-based air conditioner struggling to keep up. We quickly learned that a sunny day could turn to thunderstorms faster than a shot of Jack Daniels disappeared on Beale Street.

We booked a block of rooms for the staff and players at the historic Peabody Hotel, where at 11 a.m. and 5 p.m. a team of ducks, actual ducks, took the central elevator to and from their penthouse abode for a daily dip in the lobby fountain. The legend went that in the 1930s friends Frank Shutt and Chip Barwick came back from a hunting trip and decided to put their live duck decoys in the foundation. Apparently the two had been drinking a little too much and figured it would be funny to see them floating around in the foundation. Normally, you'd think they'd get thrown out but Frank happened to be the general manager of the Peabody. My guess is no one wanted to tell the boss how bad an idea this was but it turns out, it was actually genius. For birthdays, guests can be the Duckmaster and guide the ducks out of the elevators with a stylish hat and cane. It was also where Elvis signed his first record deal, and where, before he was famous, he window-shopped at Lansky Bros. in the lobby. If you ever wondered where Elvis got his signature look—it was from Lansky Bros.

Our weekend would begin with a Friday night fundraiser for Dontari's charity, Poe Man's Dream Foundation, followed by the camp on Saturday. We'd drive to Nashville on Sunday. Jane was supposed to take it easy, so I stepped it up to be her gofer, driver, and head coach—or rather, coordinator, since I knew next to nothing about football. Even though she was feeling better, she still had to take frequent breaks and sometimes a nap. I was thankful that Dontari and his football pals would do most of the heavy lifting.

The Friday night fundraiser was the first time I had seen Jane in a dress and make-up since she'd become sick. She glowed with a pride and radiance I had not seen since Christmas dinner 2015, right before she was diagnosed. Everyone at the fundraiser was so happy to see her.

Early Saturday morning, I blew my black referee whistle to get everyone's attention as Dontari and the other pros assembled at the front of Wooddale's cafeteria. "Listen up, everyone. Come on! Settle down!" The room fell as silent as a church right before the benediction.

We had registered over 150 kids in the previous hour, and it was time to march them to the field before we all melted in the double 95s—both temperature and humidity. But as camp director, I had to say a few words of inspiration first.

"On behalf of Dontari Poe, I'd like to welcome you to the first-ever Poe Man's Dream All-Star Camp!" A huge wave of applause, hoots, and whistles echoed through the cafeteria. It took me a minute to settle them down. "I'd now like to introduce Dontari to say a few words." More hoots and whistles.

"C'mon, y'all. Settle down!" Dontari shouted, and the room

went church-silent again. Dontari's a soft-spoken, southern gentleman type with an easy smile that's disarming given how he fills a room with his presence and voice if he wants to. "Wanted to say a few words. Be careful, it's hot. Listen to the coaches— lots of good ones here. Finally, I wanna thank Jane for making it happen. She's the reason we're doin' the camp."

Everyone looked at Jane as he gestured toward her, standing in the doorway with a huge smile on her face under a wide-brimmed straw hat, which covered her brittle hair that had slowly been growing back. Dontari had been one of the first clients we'd told about Jane's leukemia, and we continued to give him regular updates. He knew how hard she'd worked on pulling this camp together over the past six months, given all she was going through. Everyone clapped and hooted again as she started to blush.

I blew the whistle. "Let's get going." We marched out to the field. Jane mostly stayed inside the Wooddale cafeteria to escape the heat and the sun while we were all out on the field. When she did come out, it was always with a cold drink, a smile, and a bottle of sunscreen for her obsession with me not getting burned. Despite the wide-brimmed hat and ample sunscreen, the color in her face was returning, no doubt because she was taking off her hat to feel the warmth of the sun. I knew she needed it and didn't call her out on it. After a grueling four hours on the freshly mowed Wooddale pitch, we ended the camp with lunch. No one got hurt or heat exhaustion, and we all had a great camp.

THE NEXT DAY, WE ATE AT TAMP AND TAP, a hipster coffee and beer place across from the Peabody after we'd checked out and watched the ducks march out of the elevator. Jane looked happy and healthy except for the beanie, which looked out of place in the late morning Memphis sun.

Jane drove the whole two and a half hours to Nashville, more than she'd driven in six months. She smiled the whole way, singing along to Mariah Carey, her favorite, for much of the drive. At Bob and Vicky's house on the outskirts of Nashville, we planned our adventure.

"I want to take you to all my faves. There are so many." Jane rattled off the dozen or so places that we "just had to go," and she surprised me with a special reward—a "coffee shop tour." Lunch was at Pinewood Social, which made a flavorful double espresso and had a proper avocado toast and fried chicken salad to eat while we bowled strikes on their five-lane bowling alley.

Next up was Frothy Monkey, in the 12 South neighborhood, with a more granola hippie vibe. The real reason we went there, as it turned out, was because it was next door to Five Daughters Bakery. Jane bought a dozen donuts to munch on for the rest of the trip. A powerful mixture of coffee and barbecue smoke was not the smell at hipster coffee shops back in San Francisco but was an unmistakable blend in Music City USA.

On the VIP coffee tour she'd planned for me, Jane had taken great care to save the best for last. Its roll-up doors with orange and blue racing stripes along the roofline and carnival-style lettering gave Barista Parlor the feel of a throwback 1970s working man's café, which Jane knew I would like. More racing stripes adorned the central bar in a building that used to house a transmission shop, and they proudly displayed a Barista Parlor–branded anchor, auto racing flags, and an Apollo 11 capsule painted on the floor. On the far wall was the world's largest letterpress origami installation, and to cap it off, the place had an amazing collection of vinyl, mostly from the ' 60s and 70s' . Steve McQueen in *Le Mans* would have felt at home.

It was my kind of hangout—hipster mixed with the right amount of blue-collar sensibility. It's not like I was jonesing for *another* espresso, but then I heard the slurp-slurp of a barista sampling the pour-over with his silver spoon and somehow I found a place for one more.

"See, I told you this was the best one." Jane's face was a shade darker than usual because we'd been in the Tennessee sun for a few days, even though she had put on gallons of sunscreen. Chemo does make people more sensitive to the sun and they're supposed to stay out of it as much as possible, but I liked the fact that the little bit of color made her look healthier. I almost forgot that she had leukemia but was reminded when she took off her hat to wipe the sweat off her head. She smiled and nuzzled against my chest as I wrapped my arm around her. "Coffee's on me," she said.

We continued on for drinks at the Oak Bar in the basement of the Hermitage Hotel with its Italian Siena marble in the entrance, walls of Russian walnut, stained-glass ceiling in the vaulted lobby, Persian rugs, and overstuffed furniture. The art deco men's room (where you're likely to run into a group of women taking pictures) had walls of gleaming lime-green-and-black leaded glass tiles, lime-green fixtures, and terrazzo floors. We couldn't resist getting our picture taken on the two-seat shoeshine station that was right out of a 1920s mobster movie. Jane looked right at home in her flower-covered flapper-style hat, which she had started wearing because it was a lot cooler than the wide assortment of wool beanies she had accumulated over the past six months. It also made her look less cancer patient and more ironic hipster.

We didn't take any part of that weekend for granted. I was feeling rested—despite all the caffeine—and a little more normal. Jane looked and felt better than she had in months, especially in Nashville, a town she truly loved. We went home calm and ready for what was coming up next: the BMT.

From: Jane Bolander
Date: July 4, 2016 at 3:14 p.m.
Subject: Professor Klump in the Study with a . . .
To: janes-care-circle ▼

It's been a long time since we've written an update. Life has been moving ahead, and we can't believe that it's been over six months since diagnosis. I completed my third round of chemo over a month and a half ago. It was a much easier session, with only five days in the hospital this time and recovery at home. But when you're talking about chemo, it's like comparing a rotten apple to an even more disgusting and mutilated rotten apple. You don't want either of them, but one is the lesser evil.

I was in a good place when I got home because my immune system was still going down. After a few days, I started seeing bruising and petechiae, but my platelets bounced back pretty quickly. I made sure not to do somersaults around the house during that time. My white blood cells took a long time to rebound. I had the fun of a GIANT mouth sore at the corner tip of my tongue, as well as a sore in my throat, which made eating and talking near impossible for a few days. The sore's positioning was such that my tongue would rub on my teeth and mouth whenever I talked, so my tongue kept growing bigger and bigger until I became Professor Klump's twin. It was very silent in the Bolander household for a few days.

Prior to our trip to Memphis, we had a big decision to make about which donor option I am going with for my transplant, which will start around July 20.

My two options are double cord blood (umbilical cords—Stanford has reserved four cords for me) and haplo (a half match, and it would be my brother, mom, or dad). Regarding the haplo option, it was determined that my brother would be the best match for me for multiple reasons, namely because he is a younger donor (healthier cells) and there would be a one in four chance that he would be a perfect match given how genes work.

Stanford required that I make the decision between those two options or doing a national trial, which every hospital across the country is participating in. It is a randomized trial to see if haplo or cord blood would be a better donor option, with the hopes of finding that they have equal odds of survival/cure. Currently, that is what the little research shows.

My initial feeling after learning I would have to make this incredibly difficult life-altering decision on my own was one of fear, anxiety, and frustration. Bone marrow transplants have several major risks. First, you will go through incredibly heavy chemo and radiation to remove your current immune system. This is more than I have experienced before, and as you recall, my past experiences have not been very fun.

You receive a round of chemo (four days) and radiation on the fifth day while your immune system goes down to zero. On the sixth day, you receive your new cells.

You wait for those new cells to find their home and engraft into your body. This could take two weeks to a month. During this time, you live as the bubble boy with no immune system. You are susceptible to all sorts of infections and will have to be given heavy antibiotics to stave them off. Those antibiotics have their own set of fun side effects.

Not only that, the new cells could be awakened by any sort of trigger and attack your body. That is called graft-versus-host (GVHD). This is my biggest fear, as you will undoubtedly have some degree of GVHD. The "easiest" version is when your new cells attack your skin, but you could also enjoy your new cells attacking your lungs, stomach, or other organs. There is no way for us to know what will ensue until going through the experience.

Fun times.

Finally, with the help of our scientist friend, we drafted a barrage of questions for my hematologist, which included complex questions about cell density of the cord blood, the benefits of NIMA mismatches, and potential inherited food allergies from the donor cells (very important!).

We waited with bated breath for three days for a response. His thorough answers were incredibly thoughtful and insightful. No wonder he has only full five-star reviews on the Yelp for doctors.

I will share my favorite snippet below—note the smiley face!

Editorial comment:

If anyone knew which strategy is preferred, then we would all favor the preferred strategy.

If you ask us to pick, we would ask for the randomized trial as we like when possible to participate. Yet randomized trials are not for many. Take comfort in the knowledge that you have two excellent and equivalent strategies to ensure your cure :-).

Whatever you decide, we will fully support you.

It is time to come and get cured!

My heart felt full seeing the final sentence—*It is time to come and get cured!* —exclamation point and all. It instantly brought me so much hope and optimism that oftentimes falters when thinking about the hard road ahead.

I knew what I would do, and I asked Jarie, my parents, and my brother if they would support the decision. They all felt the same as me.

I'm happy/proud/excited to share that I will be participating in the national trial.

We will find out which method of transplant I will receive this coming Thursday. I'm happy to know that I can contribute to the study of BMTs for the benefit of future patients. I also know that I fully trust my Stanford team and believe in them when they say there is no option that is currently proven to be better than the other. I know they will take care of me 100 percent along the way, and I'm ready for this.

Much love,
Jane

CHAPTER 17

Pharmacology 101

B MT preparation is a pretty tricky coordination effort akin to threading a needle as you balance on a unicycle while juggling chain saws. If one thing slips, then all that conditioning chemo might have to be repeated. The genetic testing had revealed that Eric was a stronger haplo match than both Tim and Emily, which, given that we get half our genes from each parent, was good news. This meant that Eric could be the donor. For starters, Eric needed to get screened and take some immune-boosting drugs. I was impressed at how calm he was about this whole process. When we found out that he was the best haplo match, he didn't hesitate to fly out from Chicago to save his sister. Being the younger brother, I knew he looked up to her.

The typical BMT protocol took about four months to complete. The first seven days were the most intense because there were three days of prep, transplant, then the next critical four days to give the best chance of engrafting (taking hold) in the following weeks.

It had been a couple of months since they had seen each other, and when Eric arrived at the family home from the airport, he gave her a lingering hug.

"My partner in crime!" Jane said. "Thanks for saving my life." Tears had formed in the corner of her eyes.

"Of course. I'd do anything for my partner in crime." Eric's eyes were welling up with tears now too.

"How were the shots?" Eric had had to take immune-boosting shots for the past week to make sure his bone marrow had plenty to give.

"Fine. Super easy," he replied. "How are you feeling?"

"Nervous but excited to get cured." We stood there for a second, all of us with tears in our eyes, not knowing what to say or do. Eric broke the tension.

"Let me put my stuff away and then we can catch up."

The infusion had to happen the same day as the harvest itself, so if the operating room was backed up, your normal eight-hour day would be more like sixteen. That was exactly what happened.

Jane and I almost had to spend the night in the hospital and not enjoy her rising phoenix–themed re-birthday cake because it took longer to harvest Eric's marrow and longer to push it into Jane. Thankfully, we got out twenty minutes before the cutoff, which had to do with the next shift change. What a relief to sleep at our place in Palo Alto, our home away from home, and not some cramped hospital room. One thing I never wanted to do again was sleep on a chair-bed in an eight-by-twelve cramped hospital room with all the infusion pump beeps, doors opening, and handwashing.

The next four days included daily trips to the Infusion Treatment Area (ITA) for blood draws, infusions, and cleanup chemo, which is a low dose of chemo to help the patient's new immune system get a kick start. We were used to the daily trips, but the continuous IV they gave Jane made them more complicated.

"I'm sooo glad to get rid of that IV fluid. All I did was pee constantly," Jane told me as she gave back the little friend that had been with her for the last four days. The continuous

IV was a major pain for me too. I had to make sure the thing was charged and the line wasn't kinked or blocked, which was hard given that Jane had to sleep with it. The tube was always getting twisted, and when that happened it let us know with an annoying *beeeeep*. Luckily, there were no major catastrophes on my watch.

Trips to the ITA became so routine that we moved as smoothly as trains in Japan, minus the pushing, shoving, and whistles. We knew exactly when to get to the valet to avoid waiting too long. Our ITA go bag had evolved so we were fully prepared for the times when the thirty-minute trip ended up being double or even triple that length. We schlepped two laptops, three bottles of water, snacks, an extra beanie, notebooks, a hoodie, and charging cables. Sherpas on Everest carried less.

"We've been here for thirty minutes and no one has come to take my blood." Jane was busy banging on her laptop like a woman obsessed. "Can you go check to see what's going on?"

Everyone at Stanford was usually on top of everything, but for some reason, today, day five after the transplant, things were not as smooth, so I waved down Steve, our nurse practitioner.

"Hey, Steve. Jane hasn't gotten her blood drawn yet," I said as politely as I could.

"Really? I was wondering why I hadn't seen the results yet. I'll ask Kim to do it." Steve motioned for Kim to come over, then gently put a hand on Jane's shoulder and asked, "How are things going today?"

Steve was a kind man who was always friendly and extra nice to Jane.

"I'm feeling okay. Hot and my stomach has been achy for the past couple of days." Steve started to rub Jane's bald head, which was exposed because she had been feeling warm that morning. "Maybe it's GVHD," she said. "Oh. I hope not. Could it be GVHD of the stomach?"

"Hmm. You don't feel warm," Steve said as he continued to rub her head like you would rub a magic lamp or something. Maybe he was trying to get his three wishes to figure out what was wrong with her.

I could see Jane starting to spin inside her own fears. Any little pain or weirdness could lead her to spiral into the clouds, and then she'd be off to Freakoutville faster than Dorothy was carried off to Oz.

"I see." Steve was listening intently and asked if he could touch her stomach. "Hmm. When was the last time you had a BM?"

"I don't know. Like a couple of days ago. Why?"

"Sometimes people get backed up, but I can't be sure until we do an ultrasound. It could be something else, but let's see. I'll put an order in." Steve rubbed Jane's head one more time before he left, but still no genie appeared.

"What's up with rubbing my head?" Jane whispered to me.

"Maybe he was trying to feel if you had a temperature."

"That was excessive. Kinda creepy. Should I say something?"

"If it bothers you, yeah, you should. Do you want me to say something?" Jane's head was very rubbable, but it also was a little weird. I figured maybe he couldn't help himself.

"I'm gonna text Mary and see what she thinks." Jane started to pound on her iPhone the same way she had pounded on her computer, as if she were trying to smash a big hairy spider. Mary, Jane's good friend and also a doctor, was someone we'd relied on often ever since the miscarriage. She had some ideas, but it was hard to diagnose anything over text. She assured Jane that it was probably nothing but was glad we had told her about it.

I took Jane for the ultrasound on the first floor, right below the ITA. After about forty-five minutes, Steve came around to see us with a small folder of papers.

"Your labs are back, and they look like we would expect."

Steve was good at showing us all the numbers and explaining what they meant. "I also looked at your ultrasound, and it appears that you have some gas and material in your colon."

"Material? What kind of material?" Jane asked, sounding worried.

"The layman's term is 'poo.' You're constipated. What have you been eating?"

"What the sheet says to eat. Every day I have a super smoothie with avocado, spinach, Brazil nuts, almond butter, coconut water, and apple. My mom also cooks fresh veggies, rice, and some chicken." We were both relieved that it might be as simple as constipation. "What should I do?"

"I can give you a laxative, or you can drink some prune juice. That should do the trick." Steve was smiling broadly. I'm sure that was the simplest thing he'd had to deal with that day. "I'll have Roy here go over your meds and then you can go. Sound good?"

"Whew. We'll buy some prune juice."

Constipation. With all that fiber she was eating, there was no wonder she was backed up. The diet for BMT patients had to be extreme since they were losing vitamins and minerals as a result of all the medications. Jane had to have an infusion of potassium that made her ill, so instead of repeating that nightmare, we'd started her on the super smoothie. The upside was that she didn't need any more potassium infusions. The downside was constipation.

Roy was one of our regular nurses, and he knew we liked the details, especially what the counts meant, so he was thorough. "Let's go over the medications so you can get out of here." He looked at the computer screen while I looked at my one-page printed spreadsheet, which was currently at revision number five.

During BMT, the levels of certain medications are measured on a regular basis to prevent GVHD. No matter how careful you are, it's not an exact science because so many factors, including hydration, other drugs in your system, and your DNA, can cause fluctuations.

We were about to start Neupogen, a bone marrow growth factor. This would be a stomach injection, similar to the IVF hormones. When we got to that part, Roy looked puzzled.

"I don't have Neupogen starting today. Are you sure?" He was scrolling through the treatment plan, trying to make sure he hadn't missed anything.

"I'm pretty sure. That's what it says in the protocol we got." I took out my three-ring binder and handed the printed protocol to him. He appeared perplexed.

"This is the wrong one. This is for cord blood, not haplo. Where did you get this?"

"We got it at orientation." Inside I was losing it. *You* have *to be kidding me.* My temperament could go from easygoing to beast mode in one second flat ever since Jane got sick. Of all the things to worry about, we now had to worry about getting the wrong protocol.

"Did we do something wrong?" Jane asked, now on high alert.

"Not yet. The protocols are exactly the same up until now. With haplo, we wait a few more days for the injections since we gave you the cleanup chemo."

Roy left to get Jim, the resident in charge, and was back in less than two minutes.

"Hmm. This is not the right one. Are you sure you got this from orientation?" Jim was perplexed too.

"Yeah. Where else would I have gotten it?" I said, now allowing my annoyance to rise to the surface. It wasn't like I was a closet BMT doctor writing protocols in my spare time.

"Let's go over everything again to make sure you're on the right protocol. The computer says haplo, which is correct. Let's go by that." Roy, Jim, and I then went line by line through what I was supposed to give to Jane. This included thirty-plus pills and when to give her the injections. After we'd triple-checked, they let us go.

"What the hell?" Jane exploded once we left the hospital. "I can't believe they gave us the wrong protocol. Geez, what else have they screwed up?" She was furious, and her stomach hurt, and she was exhausted from the cleanup round of chemo.

"I know. We'll make sure we ask every single time. This is too important to mess up."

"What a shit show. I can't imagine what I'd do without your help. Thanks, Babesteins, for having my back. Ride or die."

"Absolutely. Ride or die," I said. "I wonder what happens to people who can't figure this stuff out. It makes my brain hurt every time."

When we got back to our Palo Alto apartment, I sent a strongly worded email to our coordinator to ask what had happened. After some investigation, it turned out that the actual file names of the documents for each protocol were so close that it was hard to tell them apart. And neither document had a title at the top! Side by side, the only way to distinguish between the two was to already know what each list should contain. Of all the things that could go wrong, to think that an unlabeled Word document would be Jane's potential demise made me ill and angry. We trusted that the doctors and nurses had it all figured out, yet like all of us, they were human and could make mistakes. Diligence and attention to detail was the only thing that saved us.

Paperwork of all kinds, including the protocol differences and medication schedules, multiplied the stress of being a caregiver. The last thing I ever wanted to do was accidentally hurt Jane or make her sicker because I misread something. My OCD rescued us more than once.

CHAPTER 18

Engraftment!

Each day Jane got stronger and could walk farther and farther around the beautiful Oak Creek Apartments in Palo Alto with her wide-brimmed straw hat, pink 3M dual filter respirator, and His & Hers sweats that had become her new uniform. Every day we'd try to go a little longer by doing one more lap around the tennis courts or walking along the creek trail, or when we were adventurous, across the street and up to the corner of Sand Hill Road and Alameda de las Pulgas.

One day we even saw another BMT couple in the same configuration, but they chose to ignore our nod and wave. Some people wanted to be alone in their struggle, or felt embarrassed by the way they looked, or didn't have the energy to socialize. Whatever the reason, we respected their decision and did not press. When her new immune system finally engrafted, it was a big deal that we wanted to share with everyone.

Engraftment was the term used when the donor bone marrow (Eric's) found its way into the patient's (Jane) bone marrow and took over. Effectively, the cells that the bone marrow was now making were from the donor. For Jane, it happened right about day twenty-six, which was typical for bone marrow transplants.

We had sent out a Care Circle update to give everyone the good news.

"Did you see all the responses?" Jane said, looking up from her laptop. "Look at all the great TV we get to watch. How fun!"

"I'm always impressed by how many people are involved," I agreed as I looked over her shoulder. Jane was clearly happy and loved reading the responses to the Care Circle update. Things had been going well since the transplant, and now that her new immune system had taken hold, we were optimistic.

"Do you think I'll live?" she asked, looking up at me, her eyes wet with tears, her face flushed, and wisps of her black hair struggling to regrow. "I don't think I could go through that again." She was smiling, but her shoulders were slumped as she looked down at the screen.

"Babe, I think so. Look how well things have gone so far." I took her in my arms as I fought to keep my own tears at bay.

We sat there holding each other for what felt like twenty minutes, during which time I finally allowed myself to just sob. We rubbed each other's backs and cried into each other's shoulders. The last eight months had been hell, but we'd survived.

We released our embrace, and Jane looked up at me. Our eyes met and she said, "I love you so much. I know this is not what you signed up for . . ."

I interjected, "No. C'mon. Don't say—"

"Wait. Let me finish," Jane said as she adjusted her glasses that were always falling down her nose. "I could not have asked for a better partner and husband. No matter what happens, I will always love you and want you to be happy. Please don't isolate yourself. People love you just as much as they love me." She then reached up and hugged me.

"I love you too. We'll get through it. Don't worry," I replied, hoping that my instincts were right.

That last part about people loving me as much as Jane took me by surprise. The thought had never crossed my mind. I was always so engrossed in the crisis of the day that I assumed all the responses were for Jane and I was just the messenger. It still felt that way, even though she said otherwise.

Jane turned back to her computer and started to read her email again.

"Look! More responses," she said, and we started to read the new ones.

The Care Circle was on fire. I guess if you ask, you shall receive, especially if it was a recommendation for TV shows to binge-watch. The Care Circle was one of the best things we did. It made things a little less scary, even though people's responses were sometimes sporadic. That depended a lot on the topic.

It was no surprise that we heard the most when we had good news to share. It was a lot easier to give a high five or to recommend a TV show than it was to commiserate over bad news. For bad news, the responses were more private in that they came in the form of texts or emails directly to Jane or me. That was understandable, since most people wanted to get more details or attempt to make sense of it all.

For me, the Care Circle gave me an outlet for my thoughts, feelings, anger, and frustration because I could write an update, review it, take out most of the swear words, and then send it out feeling that I had someplace to vent and share all the things we were going through. It felt good to be able to articulate my feelings and thoughts in a way that others could relate to. It also gave me the ability to think through the complexities of Jane's care and ensure that I didn't mess something up.

What's great about being able to share the challenges and struggles of someone's care when they're going through a health crisis is that other people can give you advice and guidance. For us, that advice was sometimes medical (there were several people with PhDs and MDs in the group), or logistical, like when everyone coordinated meals or the best brand of toothbrush or the random call to offer emotional support.

I had learned about the power of community—or lack of it, actually—the hard way during my divorce. I was glad that Jane had encouraged me to build friendships and connections. The Care Circle was the best example of the importance of staying connected and not being afraid to ask for help when needed, even though every time I asked for help, the failure lump would rise to the back of my throat.

CHAPTER 19

Booty Fit for a Pirate

After engraftment, we settled into a routine. I'd go to work Tuesday through Thursday, and Jane's parents would stay with us to make sure someone was always available for her. Jane would binge-watch *Suits* or whatever crappy USA series happened to be on. Jane's mom cooked awesome food, and her dad helped the family and Team Jane run smoothly. Her parents left us on our own most weekends to fend for ourselves like a relatively normal couple. Eric had returned to Chicago after a couple of days of recovery with no side effects from his donation other than a tender lower back where they had taken his bone marrow.

We were a tight pod of activity. We stopped doing the Care Circle updates after engraftment, figuring we were on the downhill side of everything. While it was a good sign that the new bone marrow had engrafted, I was still worried. BMT success rates were all over the map, given that the five-year survival rate hovered around 50 percent. The doctors were optimistic because of the engraftment, but they were always careful to say, "We still have a ways to go." I always found this cautiously optimistic cop-out answer less than comforting. I got their point. The odds at this point were roughly fifty-fifty. The engineer in me could work the math easily, yet the bag of emotions part of me wanted a guarantee that we were done with all this leukemia nonsense. This internal Jekyll-Hyde battle whipsawed my cortisol levels to the point that I had to take daily afternoon naps to attempt to downregulate.

Jane was going a little stir-crazy given the strict regimen she was on: pills three times a day, thirty-two in all, most of which were taken in the morning. It would take her thirty minutes to choke them all down—never fun, but essential to keep her alive.

I was proud of her dedication and commitment. Her attitude was usually pretty good unless she felt like crap. It was hard to hold a grudge against someone who, at thirty-five, was going through menopause, feeling the side effects of all those drugs, worrying about GVHD, losing all her hair, and dealing with neuropathy (tingling in the hands and feet due to nerve damage). The menopause was the hardest thing to deal with because it gave her hot flashes and mood swings that we sometimes mistook for chemo side effects. It also drove home the fact that she would never be able to get pregnant, something she so desperately wanted, and if we survived this, we'd have to pin our hopes on IVF and finding a surrogate.

"When my parents leave, can you go to Safeway and get some DiGiorno, ice cream, and Pirate's Booty? Ooh, and Sun Chips?" Jane was whispering to me as I was helping cover the PICC line with the waterproof sleeve and surgical tape so she could take a shower. She knew that junk food was not on the "recommended" parent-approved food list. "I want some junk food."

"Sure, I can hit the Safeway up the street. Your counts are going up, so you should be able to eat dairy," I said.

"Can we get two DiGiornos? One combo and one pepperoni? And also some good ice cream that has been pasteurized. It has to be pasteurized. You need to make sure."

"Got it. Hold still. We need a new one of these sleeves. It's been leaking."

"How exciting!" Jane enthused. "Labor Day weekend with junk food and tons of TV."

"Hey, hold still. I need to double-tape this or it will leak, and you'll get infected." It was hopeless. I had to let Jane have a few minutes to dance around the bathroom singing about junk food. She was becoming more like her old silly self every day.

After Tim and Emily left, I assembled our list and headed off on my mission to secure junk food. Pushing my cart down the frozen pizza aisle, I saw a familiar couple from our time at Stanford. We'd known their faces well for weeks even though we had never actually said hello, kind of like the person you see at the coffee shop every day. You nod and smile but if someone asked you their name, you'd be hard-pressed to even fathom a guess.

"You guys at Stanford?" I asked the woman who I assumed was the wife. The man had on the same pink 3M respirator Jane often wore, which was a pain to talk through.

"Yes, we are. How did you know?" she answered. They had a cart full of frozen dinners—all on the forbidden list.

"My wife is there as well. The respirator is a dead giveaway." We were members of the same exclusive club meeting out in the normal world. It was strange but also comforting.

"Oh. I'm Vicky, by the way. And this is Mark. How far along are you?" Vicky and I talked as Mark looked on, nodding his head and grunting through the respirator. She explained that Mark had a rare form of leukemia that did not respond to chemo. He was at Stanford in a last-ditch effort to get it under control. They had just started treatment and were hopeful. We wished each other luck.

Jane texted me just as I arrived in the ice cream section.

Jane: progress?

Me: Sorting out ice cream. Is Ben & Jerry's pasteurized?

Jane: oh. i don't want that. what else?

Me: There are a million different types.

Jane: picture?

I sent multiple pictures of freezers full of ice cream.

Jane: let's get three

Me: I don't see why not. I saw another couple with the respirator.

Jane: really? man or woman?

Me: Man. Nice couple. He has something pretty rare.

Jane: they talked to u.

Me: Yeah. I said hi.

Jane: oh . . . get the Talenti Caramel Cookie Crunch Gelato, Magnum Double Caramel Ice Cream Bars, Talenti Double Dark Chocolate Gelato . . . whatever you want too. :)

Me: Geez. We can't eat all that in four days. How did you know the names?

Jane: PLEASE . . . pretty PLEASE . . . did you get the pizzas? Instacart has a list. :)

Me: Yup. Two large. Got the Booty too . . . and chocolate for me. :-)

Jane: yippee! party time. Woohoo.

Jane was waiting for me at the door when I got to the apartment. "Can we make the pizza right now?" She wouldn't even wait until I put the bags down.

"Sure, but we still have all the food your mom made. We need to eat that too."

"Got it. We can have that as a snack. I want pizza. Where's the Booty?" Jane was rifling through the bags. "Nice! Woo! Party time." She ripped open the bag and took out a big handful. "Mmm. So good. God, have I been craving this! I could even taste it."

Jane ate half a bag before I put the pizza in the oven.

"You're going to get sick," I told her, worrying that she was going to overdo it given her newfound enthusiasm. "Slow down. We have all weekend."

"Easy for you to say. You can eat normal food. I know when you go 'take a phone call' at ITA, you're getting coffee and pastries. I know what you're up to." Jane had a smug smile on her face as if she'd used clever detective skills to solve the case of the snacking husband.

"I *tell* you I'm doing that. I don't keep stuff from you."

"Still, you're gone an awfully long time for a phone call. I don't mind. I know you have to decompress. The ITA can be overwhelming."

She was right. There were days when I could hardly contain my impatience with the whole process and all I wanted to do was get the hell out of the room. All those sick people—and Jane was one of them. I had an especially hard time emotionally when I got my coffee at the children's hospital across the quad from the ITA. I couldn't even imagine what it was like for those little kids and their parents.

That night after the pizza was done, we binge-watched the Japanese version of *American Ninja Warrior* on the Esquire Network and finished all the junk food.

Jane did not get sick, which was a relief. I had no idea how I would have explained that to Tim and Emily.

CHAPTER 20

Hurry Up and Wait

Eventually the trips to the ITA went from daily two-hour affairs to two times a week for barely thirty minutes as we switched from counting days to weeks after the BMT. Jane's medication also tapered off from the peak of thirty-two pills per day to fifteen, which I diligently tracked on revision thirty-seven of my Google Sheet. Her tired, sullen, irritated mood improved to contemplative, almost happy that the worst was behind us. We ventured out in the world more, including going to an outdoor movie where we ordered Red Vines and popcorn. It was the end of a tough summer, but as summer turned to fall we were optimistic that things were going the right way.

Jane's labs showed a steady improvement in both white and platelet count with the blasts still hovering around 8 percent—not great, but we were told that was normal. Her body was purging the old immune system and replacing it with the new one. All those dead cells had to get flushed out of her bone marrow via her circulating blood.

On our last trip to the ITA, about three months after her BMT, we ran into Vicky and Mark. It had been a couple of months since I'd seen them at the Safeway.

"Vicky! Nice to see you again," I said. Mark was parked in the La-Z-Boy-style infusion chair two down from where Jane was about to be set up. "This is my wife, Jane."

Vicky smiled at Jane, and Mark looked up. He was in the same kind of mask I'd seen him in before but otherwise looked completely different. He was gaunt and orangish, with sunken, unfocused blue eyes. He was around six feet tall but had clearly lost a lot of weight since I'd seen them last.

"Mark's been in the hospital for the last month and a half. It's been hell." Vicky gave me the rundown with the blank, thousand-yard, shell-shocked stare a lot of caregivers have. I recognized what she was feeling. You want to cry, but you're all cried out. "Yesterday was the first day he could get out of bed," she said, forcing a little smile. Her blue eyes were bloodshot, and it looked like she'd lost weight as well.

Mark nodded and smiled through the pink 3M respirator. Vicky told us that the doctors wanted him to keep it on because his immune system was so fragile. As Jane sat down in her infusion chair, her eyes told me she was worried. I nodded goodbye to Vicky and sat down beside Jane.

"Do you think that's going to happen to me? It looks like he has GVHD all over his skin," she whispered. GVHD was the one thing that had freaked Jane out more than any other side effect.

Graft-versus-host comes in many forms. Skin problems are the most common, followed by the stomach, then the eyes. The drug they used to control it, Prograf, needed to be carefully dosed and monitored. The trick, if you could call it that, was to suppress the new immune system enough to keep it from attacking. Give too much and the immune system would become so suppressed the patient got sick. Give too little and they got GVHD, which could be as mild as a rash or as extreme as going blind.

After our ITA appointment that day, we were signed up for a class called "What happens after BMT?" This was the graduation class, so to speak, with cancer-approved snacks and two-slide-per-page handouts, similar to those we'd received at our orientation.

We shuffled into the windowless conference room. Some patients still had their respirators on, as Jane did. Others had on their most fashionable chemo beanies or wigs, which were easy to spot. Each caregiver stood next to or behind their charge, handout and pen in hand, ready to jot down the collective wisdom about "what's next." All had the same cried-out, deep sunken eyes from lack of sleep.

Our teacher was a young Asian American woman who was one of the BMT residents. She fired up her slide deck on the ancient ceiling-mounted projector, which strained to warm up for the millionth time. It shuddered as the fan kicked in, and I was sure we'd all see it slam down in the middle of the laminated wood conference table.

"Welcome to your graduation! Congratulations on making it through your transplant." Her delivery was dry and deadpan, as if public speaking freaked her out more than the patients or death. She was clearly nervous. Her jokes were all bad and fell as flat as Kansas. Given the crowd, I thought she should have been more prepared. I guess she'd drawn the short straw.

"Now that your transplant is done, you will be transferred to the clinic where your primary doctor will watch you." She was reading right from the slides. Jane, who was a master at holding an audience during a presentation, looked at me and rolled her eyes.

We'd survived three months of hell and now faced death by PowerPoint. No wonder hospitals needed social workers to talk to the patients. Doctors were usually as awkward around patients as this woman. Patients were a puzzle to figure out, and it was sometimes hard to remember that they were also living, breathing humans. Maybe doctors imagined that all their fancy degrees would help them solve the puzzles. But I also had empathy—it had to be tough to see patient after patient, knowing some of them wouldn't make it.

The resident droned on to page four. "The most important thing to look out for is GVHD. Over the next several months, you might notice some changes in your body. Keep note of what you feel. If you have fevers, diarrhea, or skin problems, let us know." That was not on the slides and seemed important. All the caregivers wrote that down.

"As a special gift to you all, we have some hand-knitted hats, courtesy of Knots of Love. Pass them around and pick one that you like." The bag of hats came to us, and Jane picked a lovely green one. "Does anyone have any questions?"

Several of the caregivers shot up their hands, and for the next thirty minutes, all sorts of questions were hurled at our teacher. Some were silly, others serious. In an odd way, it was comforting to see all the other patients in one place.

Typically, Jane and I would roll into the ITA, whip out our laptops, and pound away at work until we were done. It wasn't that we were antisocial, but it was hard to know what to say. The normal small talk reserved for cocktail parties or work functions seemed too shallow. "Hey, what brings you here?" was obviously a stupid question. So was, "What do you do for a living?" Our jobs were to stay alive and keep our loved ones alive. Period.

After the torture of that final class, we went back to the apartment. We were leaving town the next day, so Tim and Emily had been packing. We'd still have to go to Stanford periodically and for the final test, a bone marrow biopsy, to see if the leukemia was gone, but I was excited to get back home to San Francisco and to continue Jane's recovery at our apartment.

FALL IN SAN FRANCISCO WAS THE BEST TIME. Karl the Fog (our iconic fog has been personified as "Karl" since 2010 after some anonymous person set up a Twitter account named

"KarlTheFog" and started tweeting funny/quirky things about San Francisco) had finally receded, and I remembered why I lived there in the first place.

By September we felt we were winning our campaign against leukemia. Jane's counts were generally good, and we were optimistic that the ninety-day post-engraftment biopsy would give us the news we wanted to hear: no more leukemia.

Recovery from any kind of cancer treatment is a series of forward and backward steps. There were some days when Jane left strong and wanted to walk around the block. That strength also translated to her overall mood, which made the daily work/caregiver grind a little easier. Other days, she wouldn't leave the couch unless I bribed her with CBD-laced chocolate or brought up the fact that moving her body would help speed up her recovery.

After ten months, I was finally getting into the routine of running her business, and that felt good. At least that was something I had some control over. Jane was actually impressed that JSY was on track to have its best year ever, which made her both happy and a little sad.

"How come you take over and sales skyrocket? Is it because you're a tall white guy? That must be it. Everyone is racist," she said as she texted one of her friends.

"That's not true. It's because there are two of us working on it. The more people working on the problem, the more successful. It's simple."

"When I'm better, I think you should still run JSY. I'll do the work. I love doing the work. But you can do all the management stuff, like stupid meetings, which I hate. It will be fun." She had stopped typing and looked up at me, smiling in her new green beanie from transplant graduation day.

Fun? Running a PR business is hardly fun. I found out pretty darn quickly that I'd rather have leukemia—scratch that, I'd rather go back to being an engineer.

"Can you take my temperature?" Jane stopped texting and put her hand on her head. "I'm feeling hot."

I felt her head. It was warm but not hot. I went to our go bag to retrieve a thermometer. Of all the things we could measure, temperature was the first and best indicator of problems, since when the body was fighting an infection, temperature rose to try and kill off the pathogen.

"One hundred and two. Holy shit. That's high. How long have you been feeling warm?"

"The last hour or so," she said quietly.

"We have to go to the ER. That's high."

"No. No. Please, I don't want to go back there. I hate it there. Maybe the thermometer is off. Can you use the other one?" Jane's eyes said it all. She knew a high temperature meant a possible infection, which meant the ER, which almost always led to a stay in an eight-by-ten hospital room.

"How off can it be? One hundred and two. That's way too high!"

"Use the other one. Please. I don't want to go. *Please*." Jane was clasping her hands as if she were praying to the Virgin Mary.

I grabbed another thermometer from the bathroom—one that was color coded for extra clarity.

"One hundred and one point five. Okay. That's going the right way, but it's still too high. We have to go."

"Can we wait twenty minutes and take it again? I'll drink some Ensure and water. Please. I hate it there. You have no idea." Jane was begging me with clasped hands again and tears in her eyes.

"Yes, I do know. I really do, babe. I hate it there too. The ER has those crappy plastic chairs. There's no pullout bed, so I can't sleep. There's always some newbie at the front that questions the protocol. It's not a picnic for me either, but—"

"See? We should wait. We both hate it."

Twenty minutes later, I took her temperature again.

"One hundred point eight. Better, but it's still too high. I'll take it with the other one." I put the second thermometer in her mouth and waited for the beep. "One hundred point seven. They're within point one. We *have* to go. It could be serious."

"Ugh. Fine. I'll go. Can you pack the bag? I don't feel like it." Jane slumped down on the couch as I packed our Team Jane go bag. Her face had gone slack, as if she'd heard the project she'd been working on for the past six months had gone to a competitor.

Ten minutes later, we were in the ER.

When we got admitted, the diagnosis was simple: "It looks like you're dehydrated, among other things," the doctor said. "We're going to give you two liters of fluid and some Tylenol to reduce your fever. It's one hundred point five now. We're also going to run some tests to see if you have an infection since dehydration does not explain all of this." She knew what she was doing right down to the smock, gloves, and droplet-preventing face mask. "We're also going to give you a unit of whole blood. You're a little low. That should also make you feel better."

This drill was all too common. Spike a fever. Go to the ER for fluids, anti-whatever IV drips, whole blood and/or platelets. If the fever was still high, Jane would have to be checked in. After that, we'd spend ten to fourteen days in the hospital trying unsuccessfully to figure out what was making her sick. The dehydration always frustrated Jane because she was so diligent about drinking water. The fever would go down. They would declare victory.

Leave. Rinse. Repeat.

"We're going to admit you to the hospital so we can monitor you," the nurse explained. "The fever is going down, but your counts are on the low side. We also need to make sure you don't have an infection."

Jane didn't moan or bitch. She just gave me a look of pure dread. I agreed. Another adventure on the sixth floor, more torture, more trips to my secret place, and more cornbread chicken.

If there was one skill I had learned over the previous ten months, it was the ability to just roll with it. Cancer couldn't be controlled. To get mad or frustrated by the fevers and ER visits did not help. Jane would always apologize. Like getting leukemia was her fault. That was nonsense. No one knows why anyone gets leukemia, no matter how many people want to know why.

The nurse left and Jane said, "I'm a rotten egg again. You got a rotten egg. I sometimes wish we had never met so you wouldn't have to go through this."

It was 3 a.m. and we'd been in the ER for four hours. We were both exhausted, but I hated it when she said that.

"Stop saying that. You'd do the same for me. Ride or die, remember?" I was half falling asleep in my favorite orange plastic chair. I hated the entire hospital, but there is a special place in hell for the ER. It's not made for visitors—I'm sure that's on purpose.

"I hope I don't die. I don't want to die," she said, as if talking just to herself. Then she looked over at me. "I know that you'll be sad, but I don't want you to be sad." She started to whimper and cry. I bent over to hug her. The sting of tears welled up in my eyes too. I felt so shitty and helpless, which made my failure lump appear right where I left it last time.

I'm supposed to take care of her. Protect her. I don't care if it sounds old-fashioned, that's my job as her husband, and I'm failing.

"Don't say that. We'll get through it. It will be okay. You're tough," I said half-heartedly, not because I didn't have hope but because I was worn out. Too tired. Too emotionally spent to say anything else. Ten months of this illness was getting to me. But I had to hang on and suck it up. Get out of my private pity party and roll with the cold, stinging crashing waves of fear, uncertainty, and doubt. Jane needed me. I had to focus on the task at hand—figuring out the fever so we could get back home.

"Really? You think?" She wiped her tears and looked at me. "You're telling the truth? You think I'll live?"

"I don't see why not. We've got so many MDs and PhDs on

Team Jane that we're bound to find a way. Look at all the support we have." I believed that in my heart and hoped it was true.

"Why don't you go home and sleep?" Jane suggested. "It's late, and I'll be here for a while. Come back in a couple of hours. I'll text you the room number."

"You sure? I know you don't like to be alone here." And yet crawling into our own bed was the best thing I could imagine at that moment.

"I'm sure. I'm going to get some sleep. Go home. I'll text you later." She pushed herself up and kissed my forehead. I did the same and went home to sleep with my phone on the pillow next to me.

"LOOK, BABESTEINS. IT'S OUR NEW SON, Greenie." Jane held out a green stuffed animal. "The chaplain gave him to me. Isn't he cute?"

We were on day six after our ER visit. Jane was feeling a lot better. No more fever and her counts were generally good.

"Yeah." I was not that interested in a stuffed toy but liked the smile it brought to Jane's face. "That was nice of the chaplain." This was the first time I had heard of a chaplain coming to Jane's room to visit, so that concerned me. She had been in the hospital five times before with no visits.

"Greenie has been with me all day, unlike someone else I know." Jane scowled at me to underline her point.

Greenie looked like an aging Kermit the Frog with a spare tire belly from drinking too many Bud Lights while watching Monday Night Football. He had an easy smile that was almost a smirk, like he knew something you didn't. His muted lime-green fur was halfway between the texture of a Beanie Baby and a 1970s shag carpet. I guess it wasn't easy being green after all.

"I've been out making the dollar bills, Greenie. Meeting clients," I said, feeling defensive, as I addressed our new "son."

"I know. I miss you. It's just been me and Greenie all day." Jane snuggled Greenie and started to pet his head. "Promise me you will love our son like you love me."

Jane liked to encourage what she called a "grand gesture." These were things that proved to her that you loved her—usually silly, fun things. This one was just plain odd.

"It's a stuffed animal," I said, careful not to say "*just* a stuffed animal."

"Promise me and Greenie. Go ahead. Hold him and tell him you love him as much as you love me."

I took Greenie from her and looked at him and then back at Jane a couple of times. *She is really losing it now.*

"Greenie, I love you as much as Jane and will take care of you." I quickly gave Greenie back to Jane, and she cuddled her head against the softness.

"He's happy you said that, and so am I."

Jane had never been religious. A couple of times I had taken her to St. Cyprian's, a church I attended before I met her, but that was before she got sick. Now whenever we talked about death or dying, we always said a little prayer. We figured, what harm could it do? It seemed to make her feel better.

"Can we say a quick prayer for Greenie? He would like that." Jane seemed so happy and completely sincere as she sat Greenie next to her on the edge of the hospital bed.

I tried to go with the moment. I held her hand and put my other hand on Greenie's head. "Today, we are thankful that Greenie is in our lives," I began, feeling earnest about the prayer, if not completely about my sentiments for Greenie. "He has been a welcome addition to our family. May he always be in good health. We also want to give thanks for the doctors and nurses that are helping Jane get better. They have all been kind to us. We pray that Jane's leukemia goes into remission and for help to get her through this challenging time. Amen."

"Amen. Thanks, Babesteins," she said, grinning. "Look, I got an extra meal. Your favorite, cornbread chicken."

"Yum. Did you get some extra cookies as well?"

"Yes, and pudding."

JANE WAS DISCHARGED FIVE DAYS LATER. They never figured out what had caused her fever. We rolled with it and were glad to be back home at our apartment. We were both optimistic that she was on the mend, but we had another thirty days before we could find out for sure if the leukemia was gone.

Our "son" Greenie became a permanent fixture at Jane's side. He slept between us, and she was always patting his head or cuddling him. She talked to him too, always asking if he was doing okay. And he made a semi-regular appearance in our nightly prayers. At first, I was not sure what to think of this new attachment to a stuffed animal. It was common for people to regress back to a more childlike state when the challenges of their sickness were overwhelming. This whole Greenie thing seemed a little different. She genuinely cared for him in a way you'd care for a newborn baby.

As time went on, I appreciated that Greenie would comfort her in ways that I sometimes could not. He was always there. He never asked for anything and, more importantly, never complained when she would rant and rave about the doctors or about me. I would not say I fully accepted our new son, but I did appreciate that he was a pressure release valve that would make coming back to Jane a little bit easier.

CHAPTER 21

BMT Mixed Tape

"Mrs. Bolander, we're going to do a bone marrow biopsy on you today. Do you know what that is?"

"Yes, I've had like five of them," Jane said.

It had been about a month since being discharged after the ER visit and Greenie showing up in our lives. Today was both a hopeful and a scary day because this biopsy would tell us if the BMT had worked.

Bone marrow biopsies were one of the many shitty things about blood cancer, but they were the only way to tell for sure if the cancer was gone. The biopsy consisted of drilling a hole to suck the marrow from a hip bone. This was supposed to be done under a local anesthetic, lidocaine, to numb the area so that a small tube with a funnel could be placed in the hole. The nurse or doctor then extracted the marrow while a technician took some marrow and swabbed it on a glass slide. The glass slide swab was checked to make sure they'd hit the marrow. Sometimes they hadn't and had to move to a different location—something that had happened to Jane each of the five previous times she'd had this procedure. But this was the magical ninety-day biopsy—the one that would tell us if Jane was cured or not.

"Five! So you know the procedure."

"Yeah. I'm an expert," Jane replied. "Can I play music during it? It helps me deal."

"Sure. I don't have a problem with that."

"Babe, can you set up the speaker and put Greenie next to it? The playlist is BMT on Spotify."

Jane loved the portable Bluetooth speaker my coworkers had given her. We brought it everywhere so that she could play music to take her mind off the drudgery of hospital life and for procedures like this.

"I'm going to step out. Last time it made me queasy. Will you be okay?" I asked.

"No problem. But can you stay nearby?"

"Sure. I'll be right outside." I bent down and kissed her forehead, fired up the playlist, and left.

In addition to hating the smell of hospitals, I had always hated seeing blood. Every time I got a blood test, I'd have to psych myself up so I wouldn't pass out, which included deep breaths and closing my eyes so I wouldn't see my life fluid drained from me. Giving blood was even worse. When I was sixteen, I tried it, turned white, and nearly fainted, and that was the end of my blood drive days.

The last time Jane had this type of procedure, I'd made the mistake of looking over at the funnel sticking out of her biopsy tramp stamp to find blood spurting out. I nearly lost my double espresso and orange glazed scone.

I hoped this time would go more smoothly, but as soon as I had that thought I heard Jane protesting through the door and over the music. "Ouch. Ouch! I can still feel it. Ugh. Are you done yet?" A couple of nurses rushed past me with worried looks on their faces. Jane had a high tolerance for pain, but I could tell by her voice that she was hurting.

"Almost done. A few more minutes."

"It hurts. Please hurry up," Jane pleaded.

I paused near the door, unsure what to do. I was angry they were hurting her and wanted to barge in and figure out what the fuck was going on, but I knew that could make the situation worse and cause it to take longer. I decided to sit there, listening to Jane moan, and wait for them to finish.

As soon as the nurses got the sample, I went in. "What happened?"

There was silence. It was probably only a minute but felt like an hour. Jane had tears in her eyes and was grimacing.

"I could feel it. I don't think they gave me enough lidocaine. Babe, it really hurts," she explained, starting to cry.

I looked at the doctor and the nurse. "What the hell? She could feel the whole thing."

The answer I got was standard PR speak.

"We gave her the prescribed amount. I don't know why she felt it. Maybe we didn't go deep enough."

Had the doctor not been a woman, I might have hit her.

"Don't you think you should know? She's been through like five of these, and this has been the worst one. What are you going to do about it?"

One of the things I hated about the health-care system was the lack of accountability. People needed to fucking admit when they screwed up. Shit happened, and I got that. But to deny it or give me some bullshit excuse made the whole thing more unbearable.

"I'm sorry, Jane. I don't know what happened." The doctor was looking at Jane, avoiding eye contact with me. "We can give you some pain meds to make it feel better. We did get the sample, so we don't have to do it again. It was hard to extract."

"Yeah. Give me some meds. It really hurts." Jane was still crying.

After the pain meds took over, she relaxed a bit. By the time we were released, she was feeling much better. As I wheeled her to the car, she whispered, "I hope the cancer is gone. I don't think I can handle another biopsy like that. It was torture."

From: Jane Bolander
Date: January 5, 2017 at 12:17 p.m.
Subject: Update a Year after Diagnosis
To: janes-care-circle ▼

Happy New Year Friends,

It's been a while since we've had an update, so here I am!

A few days before Christmas, I had another bone marrow biopsy.

It happened to be the biopsy from hell, cuz the nurse practitioner most likely didn't go deep enough with the numbing med. I could feel every inch of the needle digging into my marrow, and my whole body started trembling uncontrollably. I could barely make it through, but somehow did. Our bodies are strong when there is a will to survive.

The results came back the Friday before Christmas Eve. The cancer blasts unfortunately grew from 8 percent prior to chemo to 30 percent, which means my cancer has taken over my donor cells.

We've learned that the cancer has evolved so it either is able to hide its markers from my donor cells or it emits a "fragrance" that causes my donor cells to "sleep" instead of attacking the cancer. It was time for a new approach.

After a great meeting with my Stanford doc, the plan is chemo, which started at Santa Clara Kaiser yesterday, followed by a boost of my brother's donor cells in two weeks and then a dose of a new "avant-garde" drug, Keytruda, that blocks the cancer's ability to hide from my immune system. This drug has rarely, if ever, been used on leukemia patients but has been very effective on lymphoma and lung and neck cancers.

We also learned some good news from a chimerism blood test that my donor T-cells are at 90 percent. T-cells are the fighter cells that battle the cancer, so this course of treatment, being the chemo plus the boost of donor cells, is definitely the way to go. Jarie said that I've always been one to enter uncharted territories, so perhaps it's fitting that this new path will get me to a cure. I feel really good about this one.

Thank you for all of your continued support and thank you for reading. It has helped so much. I'm currently typing away on my lovely new computer, which I'm SO grateful for! I love typing and texting during the day and binge-watching in the evening. :)

Love,
Jane

CHAPTER 22

Update a Year After Diagnosis

Once we realized that the BMT had failed, Jane thought it best for her to send out the Care Circle update. She spent the better part of an hour writing and rewriting what to say. Usually, she would ask me to read it before she sent it out, but not this one. I read it when everyone else did.

No one responded directly to the thread like with good news; they texted or called instead. The support felt good, but she was depressed that she was running out of options. I could see it in her face every time she got to the point where she explained the set of options to whichever friend was calling her. Her voice changed, and her eyes and mouth drooped. Sometimes she cried.

The cancer journey with Jane was like being in the middle of the ocean—a no-man's-land where the distance between me and the shore was too far to cross before the next wave crashed against me. The only real option was to go deeper so the waves would stop overwhelming me. But the problem was the deeper I went, the more tired I got, and the less chance I had to return to shore. This pushed me to go deeper and deeper to try to catch my breath.

We were pushing into the deep blue ocean of options to cure Jane. None of them were good, and all of them had their own complications. None were guaranteed, and all brought more suffering.

I was vaping twice as much CBD to sleep and having at least three, sometimes four double espressos to combat the mental and physical fatigue from the yearlong campaign to keep Jane alive. It was hard to stay focused and even harder to discuss treatment plans, talk about how JSY was going, and stay on top of all the medications. I also felt guilty that I was mad about the whole bullshit cancer thing. I never imagined that a little over a year into our marriage we'd be battling leukemia together.

Friends would ask how things were going, and I'd say, "Fine." For me, it was better to hide the pain than to deal with it or explain it. I knew that most people didn't want to talk about it anyway. It was depressing to go over the details and feel the tragedy of a young woman getting leukemia and battling for her life. If I did talk about it with someone, we focused on how Jane was coping. Occasionally, someone would ask, "How about you?"

In a critical illness, I was dealing with it 24/7. I didn't have any days off. All my physical energy, mental fortitude, and free time went to saving my loved one's life. Nothing else mattered, and that was how I could get into trouble.

The beautiful thing about how Jane and I dealt with her illness was that she made it a point to give me space for me. Not a lot, but it was enough to maintain my sense of self, not just "Jane's husband, Jarie." Believe me when I say that matters more than you might think.

Other than getting enough sleep and eating well, taking time apart from Jane and focusing on myself were the best things I, as a caregiver, could do. I struggled a lot with both.

The intensity of the emotions that welled up every day during a long battle with cancer was overwhelming. In that oceanic no-man's-land, each wave that hit prevented me from catching my breath. And if I did get a moment's rest, I felt guilty because Jane was still treading water, trying not to drown.

Cancer made me feel helpless, alone, and anxious, all while I knew I was supposed to be an emotional rock for the person I loved. How dare I feel cheated out of my own life when my wife might die? That inner conflict was hard to share with people, hard for anyone to really hear. But it was harder to deal with in my own head. The guilt of feeling cheated out of a normal life made some of my days pure pity parties of epic magnitude.

As time went on, our support network started to slip away because I didn't want to talk to our friends about the state Jane and I were in. We still had the Care Circle, but the updates were less and less frequent. I didn't do what a good friend should do—reach out and engage. The only consistent support groups in my life were Jane's parents and my workout group.

I had found the workout group after my first wife, Margaret, left me. Those people and our shared activities were the only constant in my life for years. Physical movement saved my soul and my sanity more than once. There was no better therapy than slinging weight like a meathead. Henry Rollins, in his 1994 *Details* magazine article entitled "Iron and the Soul," put it perfectly in the last paragraph:

> *The Iron never lies to you. You can walk outside and listen to all kinds of talk, get told that you're a god or a total bastard . . . Friends may come and go. But two hundred pounds is always two hundred pounds.*

Doing some mindless weight slinging regulated my body's response to stress. The weight did not care about my troubles. It was there to be lifted and couldn't give two fucks about my mood. The weight did not judge or show pity. It was present and waiting, with no agenda. And it didn't spare my feelings like people always wanted to do.

It wasn't that friends and family intentionally lied to me when we were going through Jane's battle with cancer. But people treated us differently. They didn't tell us certain things because it might upset us or because they felt we had enough on our plate. At times that was welcome and necessary, but it did cut us off from the real world. The longer we were cut off, the harder it was to relate to "normal" people and feel normal ourselves. Shielding those who are going through a challenging time from worries may seem like the right thing to do, but there can be unintended consequences. I felt more and more alienated and awkward around my friends and family because the cancer elephant in the room was always looming.

The most vivid example of someone trying to spare my feelings during Jane's illness was when my mother found out she had breast cancer six months into Jane's leukemia treatment. My parents didn't want to tell me for obvious reasons: "Jarie has enough to worry about."

The original recommendation for my mother was a mastectomy, even though it was stage 1 breast cancer. If I'd learned one thing about health-care professionals, it was that you should always feel free to question them and challenge things that make no sense. After she finally told me about her situation, I suggested my mom get a second opinion from the oncology team that was treating Jane. They recommended a lumpectomy, no chemo, and no radiation. For her age and stage, that made way more sense. I felt a rare sense of victory and was pleased that I could apply what I had learned to help my mom. Still, I was frustrated that she'd waited so long to tell me.

Our family and the few friends who would tackle the realities of what I was dealing with and acknowledge how fucked up it was were a huge help. Still, most of the time, I felt I shouldn't talk about it. What right did I have to complain? I wasn't the one with cancer.

Eventually, it was easy to descend into self-medication and isolation, easier to spend all my time in my own private pity party rather than explain how I was feeling to people when I didn't even want to think about it myself. This was especially true for my family. We were brought up to not rely on anyone or ask for anything. Sure, we'd ask for help for mundane things like trips to the dump or moving furniture, but never for something so emotional. That was why during the past year I might have seen my parents and two brothers two or three times max at family get-togethers, and the one time I went with my mom for the second opinion.

We did talk on the phone often, but it was never more than, "How's Jane doing?" To be fair, they did try, but I was so wrapped up in the mission to save Jane that I could not bring myself to ask for, let alone accept, help. Not that I didn't want it—I just had no way to ask for it that did not put the burden on me to figure out what help I needed.

CHAPTER 23

A Gift from Patty

*K*nock. *Knock*. "Hello. Is it okay if I come in?"
We were two days into Jane's current round of chemo. She had been transferred to Santa Clara Kaiser because all inpatient chemo would be done there.

I thought it was a major pain in the ass to go down to Santa Clara, forty miles away from our home in San Francisco. The upside was that the rooms were nicer, the pullout bed more comfortable, and everyone in our wing had cancer, so the nurses were all experts. A huge help.

"Come in," I said.

"Hi. I'm Patty. I wanted to drop by and say hi. I'm your social worker. I usually like to come to see new patients." Patty had a grandmotherly way about her even though she looked to be only in her midfifties.

"I don't think we really need to talk to a social worker," Jane replied. "I think we're good."

"Oh. Okay. I'm sorry." Patty smiled and turned toward me. "I didn't get your name."

"Jarie. I'm Jane's husband." I was on the pullout chair, which was tucked into the opposite corner from the door.

"Nice to meet you. Do you stay with Jane at night?"

"Yeah, I sleep on this thing."

"How's that?" Patty asked. "It must be uncomfortable."

"Not as bad as the ones up in San Francisco. Those are awful." I smiled. I liked this woman. She wasn't condescending and seemed sincerely interested in talking with us.

"He stays with me whenever I'm in the hospital." Jane looked up from her laptop again. She glanced at me and set the laptop on her movable dinner tray, next to Greenie.

"That's nice of him. It must be hard to sleep here," Patty said.

"It's not that bad. I usually vape some CBD, put in earplugs, and wear a sleeping mask. This place is a lot quieter than San Francisco."

"Yeah," Patty laughed. "It certainly is. I also hear that the rooms are bigger here."

"Much bigger and cleaner," Jane piped up. She was now sitting upright in her bed.

"Who is this?" Patty pointed to Greenie.

"That's Greenie. The chaplain in San Francisco gave him to me." Jane's face lit up with a smile. Her fuzzy green child. Her partner in crime. The one thing that had constantly been with her and she loved and cared for dearly. It was strange to say and even stranger to feel, but I was thankful for Greenie since he gave her so much joy.

"So cute. He must give you a lot of comfort."

"Yeah. He keeps me company when Jarie leaves." Jane picked up Greenie and gave him a hug.

"Well, I know you guys don't want to talk, but it's a policy that I come by and introduce myself. I know it's getting late and all. Is there anything that I can get you, or questions I can answer? I can also come back tomorrow."

Before Patty knocked on the door, Jane and I had been having an emotional discussion about what would happen if she died. She was worried about me being sad and how I would get along afterward. I hadn't really wanted to discuss it because I didn't want to think about that possibility. I was doing my best to stay positive and on task, but the negative thoughts were creeping in more and more since we'd discovered the BMT had failed. But when Jane herself brought up the subject of dying, I always lost control.

"I actually have a question." I turned to Patty on impulse, blurting out, "How am I supposed to deal with her talking about if she dies?" Even saying those words, "if she dies," was excruciating.

"Oh. That's a big one. Can I come in and sit down?"

"Sure." I pulled an extra chair over near the bed and continued, "It really frustrates me when she talks about dying and says that we should never have met. She's worried about me being sad if she goes." I suddenly felt I had permission to say things I had tried not to say to anyone for weeks and months. This was Patty's job, right? She was there to listen to stuff like this. Maybe she could give me some tools to deal with all of it. I was trying to hold back my tears, but they were coming anyway.

"I don't want you to be sad, okay?" Jane said. "I know it's going to be hard on you and my parents. I want you to be happy. It *would* have been better if we never met." Jane's eyes were filling now too.

"How can you say that? That's not cool at all." My voice rose a little higher as I kept trying to hold it together. "You're always saying that stuff. I hate it."

Patty was now seeing the truth, not our polite smiles and small talk. This was where we'd left off before she came in. She waited until we paused for breath and said, "It's common for couples to think about this. It's only natural that a happily married couple will worry about each other, care about what happens to each other. Why does it frustrate you when she talks about that?" It was almost as if she'd planned this whole interaction.

"She is going to get better," I said. "We have to figure out how to cure her. We don't have to worry about what happens later. Focus on the task at hand. Don't get sucked into the negativity of all this." I had been talking to Patty, but now I looked directly at Jane. "You're not a rotten egg."

"I know that you'll be sad if I go. I worry about that, all right? I don't want you to be sad your whole life. I want you to find love again." Jane's voice was uncomfortably loud and high-pitched now. She was yelling and crying at the same time.

"I don't want to talk about you dying. *That* makes me sad." I was so frustrated that my fists were clenched and shaking. All this talk had been simmering for a while. It had started in Palo Alto but had intensified lately. I could feel us moving into a shouting match as Patty leaned toward Jane.

"It's okay to share your feelings about this." Patty's voice was low and soft as she tried to calm the tension in the room. "Most happily married people want to find love again after losing their partners. In fact, most survivors find a new partner quickly, especially men. Usually within the first year. Happy people want to be happy."

That bit of information was irritating. Did she think I was going to run off with some new girlfriend the minute Jane wasn't around?

"Can we stop talking about this now?" I asked. I wanted Patty to go away.

"No. I want to talk about it some more," Jane replied. She'd stopped crying. "I'm the one that's dying. *Not you.* I get to talk about this if I want to. I want to make sure you and my parents don't get sad if I go." She was steadfast. And this was her brand—Jane always wanted to make sure the details were taken care of and buttoned up.

Patty leaned farther forward and put her hand on the bed near Jane's. "Jane, of course they will be sad. They love you. When we lose a loved one, we get sad. It's part of life. If you love, you will lose. That loss will make you sad."

Patty was so matter-of-fact in her calm, grandmotherly voice. She hesitated a moment, then added, "The best that you can do for the people you love is enjoy the time you have together. A lot of how those who survive deal with loss depends on the way the dying person dealt with it."

"What do you mean?" Jane said before I could.

"Well, how you, Jane, handle your life now will help the people you love deal with whatever happens later. Jarie, I know this is tough to talk about, but it's good that you know that Jane wants you to be happy. *That's a gift.*"

I thought about that for a second. A gift. My wife told me she wanted me to be happy and find love again if she died. That was supposed to be a gift to me. I'd never thought about it that way, and it took a little while to process.

"Jarie, the way you handle this part of your life will help Jane as well. If she knows that you will be okay, that will make her happy and bring her peace. Do you see how this works? I know it's hard to grasp, but *accepting* whatever is going to happen and talking about it, planning it, living in the moment, being happy, being sad, will truly make it better."

Jane looked me in the eye. I had gotten up and moved beside her bed while Patty was talking. I was holding her hand. She squeezed it tight.

"I want you to be happy because you make me so happy." Jane's tears were impossible for her to stop now. "Ride or die, remember? Even if I die, I'm still on the ride with you, always."

"I know. You make me happy too," I replied. "Don't feel like you're a burden or that this is hard. I'll be here until I can't be here anymore. I'll do my best to be happy no matter what. I love you."

"I love you too."

Patty stood up. "I'm going to go now. If you need anything, here is my card." She dropped a simple white business card on the tray next to Greenie. "Jane, I hope you get better soon. Jarie, keep it up. Both of you are doing great."

CHAPTER 24

A Little Help from My Friends

"Hey, Jarie. It's Greg. I just wanted to call to catch up and see how you're doing today." That's all my friend's message said, and I listened to it a few days after he'd left it, but it was a real lift to hear his voice.

I had recently shut off every notification on my phone. I never wanted the stupid thing to go off in the middle of the night or during an important appointment. Truth be told, I also hated the fact that I was beholden to those beeps like a trained rat that pushes the lever for more cocaine-laced water.

It was February 2017, and Team Jane had been on the leukemia adventure for thirteen months. We were about to embark on a new experiment, which would be the last shot at curing Jane.

Greg was a friend I had met after a talk I did about writing creative nonfiction. He was a corporate burnout who wanted to find more meaning in his life. He'd successfully left his eighty-hour-a-week job and wanted to help others do the same. He was taking the same class I'd taken to figure out how to write a book about work-life balance. The teacher had asked me back to talk about the process. Jane had been Greg's publicist on his first book, *Busting Your Corporate Idol: Self-Help for the Chronically*

Overworked. We had hit it off right away and had coffee at least once a month to compare notes on writing and life.

I called him back three or four days after he left the message. "Hey, Greg. It's Jarie. Sorry for not getting back to you sooner, man. I just got your VM," I said when he picked up after the third ring.

"No problem. No problem at all. How've things been going?" Greg had a calm and soothing voice, the meditative kind that could put you to sleep, but in a good way. I always imagined that when he read bedtime stories to his two daughters, they never got past the first couple of pages.

"Honestly, things aren't going well at all," I shared. "Jane's really sick and not getting better." I don't know what came over me. Usually, I'd have given anyone who asked my usual PR response and gotten off the phone. For some reason, today was different.

"I see. Wow. That's got to be tough."

"I'm sorry. I need to unburden my soul of this, Greg. I don't think she is going to make it." The floodgates had opened. With Greg, that was easy since we had talked a lot about life during our coffee chats. I could trust Greg to be able to handle what I needed to get off my chest. "The leukemia is out of control. Nothing they are doing is working. She's getting sicker and sicker. I have no idea what to do. It fucking sucks. I feel helpless." I started to cry for real, like I did when I was alone.

"Are you sure that it's not helping? The last email sounded upbeat." Greg was a member of Jane's Care Circle and was always responding with words of encouragement.

"You know Jane. Always wanting to spin things to look good. But it's not good at all. The cell boost helped a little, but the cancer cells are still there. We're going to try this Keytruda experimental drug that's never been tried before on leukemia. It's supposed to activate the new immune system. UC Irvine told us about some plant extracts that are supposed to help. We're trying to up the dose on the pot. Shit, man. Literally nothing is working."

I could hear how hopeless I sounded, and part of me wanted to walk it back, to say something positive. But it also felt good to finally tell someone the truth about how I felt. I kept crying.

"Well. You're doing all you can, man. What else can you do?"

"I don't know. Maybe go to another hospital or clinic." I wiped my eyes and nose on my sleeve. "All these docs stay in their lane. It's amazing that we're doing the Keytruda. Dr. Lee is actually pretty aggressive. He's even looking into other clinical trials. It's too much, man. Too much to handle. I can't handle this anymore." That last part I hadn't admitted to anyone, including Jane's parents and mine. I had felt a couple of times that I was about to snap, but as far as anyone else knew, I was the model husband, stoically caring for my sick wife.

"You don't need to handle this all on your own. People have been helping, haven't they?" Greg asked.

"Yes, but it's hard for people to understand. I'm not going to give up or anything like that. No way. No how. Fuck this whole leukemia thing. It's so fucked up. She does not deserve any of this. No one does. You should see all the people at Stanford. All colors. All walks of life. There was this young Indian couple we saw the other day. They looked just like us. Leukemia does not give a shit who you are." My tears were starting to dry up, and it felt good to vent all my frustrations.

"I know people say this to you a lot . . ." Greg paused, probably worried that I'd start yelling or crying again. "But is there anything I can help you with?"

"Just listening to me rant is great. I know you really want to help. I get that people don't know what to do. I never knew what to do myself. I don't blame anyone. They try. It's just so frustrating to have to manage all this. Fuck. Fuck. This is so fucked up. Sorry, man."

I had started to calm down. This was familiar to me. I had to get mad at a problem in order to tame it. I told Greg how much I appreciated just being able to lay it all out there with him.

"It's easy to listen," he said. "That I can do. Can't cook worth a shit, but I can listen."

We both laughed, and that felt good too.

"Why don't we chat every couple of weeks?" he offered. "Nothing too formal. We don't even have to talk about Jane or leukemia. Just shoot the shit."

"Yeah. That would work. Sometimes I want just five minutes of alone time to not worry about her drugs or fevers or appointments or answering someone's question. Thanks a lot."

"Okay, we have a plan. Plans are good. Something to look forward to."

"Yup," I agreed. "I love it when a plan comes together."

We spent the rest of the time on the phone catching up on his family, random stuff about books and TV—and not talking about leukemia. It was an hour of normalcy. You don't realize what normalcy is until it's taken away from you. It sounds crazy, but being treated like a normal person with mundane problems and complaints felt great, because I didn't feel so alone. It was comforting for me to finally relate to another person with some common life challenges that didn't involve obsessing about my wife's health, and whether there was anything I could do differently to ensure she'd survive.

CHAPTER 25

The Last Waltz

"I brought you a surprise!" Erin shouted as she opened the door to Jane's parents' house. Erin was a friend of Jane's who had flown in to visit from New York. "I know how much you like Atelier Crenn, so I spoke to them, and they made you a picnic. Dominique Crenn did a video for you. She's in France, but I told her about you, and she wanted to say something."

"Aw. That's so sweet. I'd hug you, but I can't right now." Jane was standing in the hallway as Erin and their friend Sarina entered the room. This was the second friend visit in as many days. The day before, Ria and Mary had come by to catch up, chat, and see how Jane was doing. Jane had reached out to Mary to organize visits because, according to the doctors, we were in uncharted territory. In a few weeks, Jane might not be well enough to have visitors.

"Don't worry about it. Also, the food is all cooked, nothing is raw. I made sure of that," Erin said.

We all sat down on the sofa while Emily got plates and water. Erin pulled out her phone, and we saw Chef Crenn in a field under the shade of a tree, in what looked like the South of France. She apologized for not being able to make the food herself. She hoped Jane enjoyed it and got better soon. It was a sweet gesture that made Jane smile.

"That was so nice of her. Thanks, Erin, for setting things up," Jane said.

"Anytime." Erin grinned as she put some treats on her plate. We all started munching on brioche and preserves. "How's things, Yinster?"

"So-so. We're doing the Keytruda thing now, and it makes me tired and itchy." Jane's words were measured. Her voice was softer than usual, and she moved slowly and deliberately to grab her glass of water and the plate her mom had prepared for her. "This is so good. I want to eat it all."

"Take it slow," I warned her, but she just looked at me with a smirk.

"Okay, *Mom*. Between you and my real mom, I can't have any fun." It was a jab, but it was funny too—and also true.

"I'm looking out for you," I replied, playing along. "You just got out of the hospital. Do you want to go in again?"

"Party pooper." Jane smiled and popped another bite of brioche in her mouth.

The food was excellent and cheered Jane up. She loved feeling special enough to have a picnic designed just for her.

"When do you go back to San Francisco?" Sarina asked.

"In the next couple of days. I have to get another dose of Keytruda."

We talked for another twenty minutes or so until Jane got tired. A half hour was her limit at that point. We'd warned her friends in advance, so there were no surprises about her lack of energy.

"I'm going to nap. You guys can stay for as long as you like. Thanks for coming and bringing the food. Delish," she said as she got up.

I helped Jane go back to her room, and when I returned, Sarina and Erin were getting ready to leave.

"I'm so glad we could see her, and you as well. We can come back anytime if she can take visitors," Sarina said as she and then Erin hugged me goodbye. "She looks pretty good." Sarina nodded. I knew the look she gave me was saying, *Tell me she's going to be okay.* It was the same look Mary and Ria had given me the day before, although their faces had been more somber.

Mary was a pediatrician, and she had been helping us get referrals and understand all the drugs, blood tests, and protocols. Mary fully understood the seriousness of what was happening, and I was glad to have someone like that to rely on. She had such a calm demeanor and a husky-sweet voice that put my mind at ease. I always felt better after talking to her, and so did Jane. After the endless phone calls with her, I now understood why Jane called her Mother Mary.

I paused, trying to decide how to address Sarina's unspoken question. "Jane's handling the Keytruda okay. It makes her tired and itchy, and she forgets things. She's also on a dozen meds, and they all have all sorts of side effects. All in all, not too bad, but not great. Let's hope it kicks in and starts to work."

"Keep us posted," they said as they left, waving and smiling.

I'm not sure why I didn't go ahead and tell them how serious Jane's condition was. I guess part of me was still in denial. I didn't want to give up. And Jane's parents were there, which made it harder.

My most difficult job at that point was talking with Jane's parents. I was the one who had to relay what the doctors said, and I was always cautious, careful to make sure I got the details straight and stayed calm and composed for them. We always made all the decisions as a team, which comforted me and relieved a little of the pressure I was feeling.

There were other visits scheduled after Erin and Sarina, but Jane decided to cancel them.

"I don't feel like seeing anyone else. It takes a lot out of me," she told me when I walked into the room where she was resting after Erin and Sarina left.

"Got it. You don't have to do anything you don't want to."

"Thanks. I want to rest. I saw everyone I wanted to see." This was a change from the week before when she had scheduled at least thirty such friend visits. We never acknowledged it, but she seemed resigned to the fact that these final few visits would be the last ones she'd have with her friends.

THE NEXT COUPLE OF DAYS WERE SPENT relaxing in Walnut Creek. We had an appointment at Stanford the next week, followed by another Keytruda infusion. That meant we'd be spending most of our time at our apartment in San Francisco.

Jane's mom had offered to come and help us out because Jane had trouble walking on her own. We were now using a wheelchair to cart her around. At home, we routinely helped her to the bathroom and stayed close in case she couldn't get up. Eating was more difficult for her too, despite all we did to make sure her favorite treats were on hand.

The blood and platelet transfusions were more frequent, and her counts were all over the place after the second Keytruda treatment, but that was expected. If she could hold on through the lulls, the doctors thought maybe the cells in combination with the Keytruda would take hold. If that happened, Jane would be cured, and we could eventually get back to a more normal life.

If the Keytruda and the new cell infusion didn't work, the backup plan her parents and I had chosen was to apply for several promising clinical trials out of UC Irvine. These trials took drugs similar to Keytruda that were used for solid tumors and gave them to leukemia patients.

At that time, we were also ramping up Jane's doses of Rick Simpson Oil, a high concentration cannabis extract, and some other plant extracts—including turkey tail mushrooms—that had shown promise in limited trials.

We would try anything we could to keep Jane alive.

CHAPTER 26

If I Know What Love Is,
It's Because of You

"I can't really do anything for you," the doctor said. "You're too sick." Jane and I had driven down to Stanford to get some advice on what the next steps were.

"Too sick" seemed to be an understatement. Within the past week, we had been to half a dozen appointments for platelet infusions, a couple of pints of whole blood, the eye doctor for scratched retinas, and lung function tests, which explained why she could barely walk down the hall. We all knew that, but to hear that the guy with all the letters after his name could do nothing for her was a punch to the gut that unleashed new waves of emotion that crashed over us like a tsunami. It was the end of March, and while we thought the Keytruda had helped in some ways, the leukemia and the GVHD were now out of control, the doctor explained.

We needed another plan.

The drive home from Stanford was tense, at least for me. Jane was tired but still seemed optimistic in the way you're optimistic about winning the lottery. Sure, the odds were against us, but someone had to win—it might as well be us. She had closed her eyes. She'd woken up again with scratched retinas that morning, so it was painful to open them. That was our first clue that graft-versus-host had begun.

"Maybe we can go to LA," she said. "The UC Irvine docs seem to think they can help."

"Yeah, we can also do all the alternative stuff they recommended. Let's call them and sort it all out," I said. We were racing up I-280, back to our apartment in San Francisco.

Jane's mom had been staying with us for the past couple of days, and I appreciated having the help. As a caregiver, my whole life revolved around appointments, drug schedules, cooking, cleaning, and getting the extended network of friends and family educated and informed. It was taxing, and Jane's mom was great about pitching in and doing whatever we needed.

"Hey, Mom. The news is not good," Jane told her before I could even get her coat off. We had come home to an apartment filled with the smells of a delicious dinner. "The doc said he can't do anything for me. The GVHD is out of control, and I need to take steroids to get it back under control." Jane had tears in her eyes. Her mom started to tear up as well.

"Don't steroids make leukemia worse?" Emily asked.

Jane nodded. "I don't have a choice. No one will treat me if the GVHD is this bad," she explained.

"Okay," Emily managed. "So, what do we do?"

"We can start the Rick Simpson Oil and the supplements that UC Irvine told us about. When she improves, we can head down to LA and do one of the clinical trials," I said with as much confidence as I could muster.

THE STANFORD VISIT WAS ON MONDAY. We talked to our Kaiser doc about alternatives on Tuesday, and by Thursday he delivered the same prognosis, based on the combined labs from Stanford and Kaiser. They couldn't do anything more for Jane.

She might have a few days or a few weeks. It was hard to say for sure, because leukemia affects people in different ways.

Jane's brother, Eric, arrived from Chicago early in the evening on Thursday. She stayed up to say hello but then went right back to sleep.

Friday and Saturday were a blur. Jane stayed in bed most of the time. She was tired and hardly said a word. She only got up once to go to the bathroom. She was weak but still managed to blow me a kiss and crack a smile, which gave me some hope. I told myself that Jane was the toughest woman I had ever met and that she was still fighting. I loved her so dearly, and I prayed she could fight her way back to me. I knew it was a long shot, but hope was all I had at that point. There was nothing more I could do for her. I had to accept whatever happened.

On Sunday, Jane's dad told me he would take the first shift so I could rest. We had divided taking care of Jane into four-hour shifts between the four of us once Eric got into town. That way, each of us could have at least twelve hours to sleep, run errands, or decompress. Sleeping next to someone who was so sick was emotionally draining. We didn't sleep much. The whole night was filled with the sounds of Jane's labored breaths. Again and again, we wondered if this breath or that one might be the last. The spikes of cortisol rose and fell like the waves against a sea wall, with the occasional one that found the right crack to drench us.

For me, cannabis was a savior. I would often vape a CBD-heavy concentrate to relax enough to get three or four hours of consistent rest. It worked much better than booze, and without the suspicious looks from my in-laws, because they had no idea what I was doing.

The first shift on Sunday was from 10 p.m. to 2 a.m. We set it up that way because we had to give Jane liquid morphine at midnight, a last-minute addition to the host of drugs for Jane's comfort.

Jane slept in our bedroom, and whoever was not on duty (her father, mother, brother, or me) slept on an inflatable air bed in our living room.

As Tim's shift started on Sunday night, at 10 p.m., I escaped to the bathroom to toke up some CBD extract to help me fall asleep. My shift started at 2 a.m.

I awoke at 1:30 a.m., thirty minutes before my shift, to Jane's labored breath. For a moment, I was paralyzed with fear. Her breaths were short and irregular, like a muted snore. I struggled to regain my composure. The fog of my half dozen CBD vapes made it hard to focus. I still felt like I was dreaming. Finally, after a good five minutes, the dread spurred me to roll off the air mattress I was sharing with Eric and cautiously go into our room.

"Close the door," Tim said as I entered. He was kneeling by her side, holding her right hand. Jane held Greenie in the crook of her left arm with his head turned toward her face, as if he were watching over her, along with Tim and me.

I was still foggy from waking up and could not focus in on the dim light of the alarm clock and night-light. Tim was mumbling something over and over again that took me a couple of seconds to hear.

"Everything will be okay. I love you. Go to the light," he said. He repeated this several more times as we hovered there, keeping watch.

She was close. You could hear it in her breath. It sounded like her lungs were full of fluid, which made her sporadically gasp. When she did that, her body arched and Greenie moved back and forth along with her, periodically raising her right hand to scratch her nose.

I kneeled beside her. Grasping Jane's other hand, I told her, "I love you. I'll be okay. Go to the light."

We kneeled there for what felt like hours, taking turns saying the "go to the light" manta over and over again. Tim and I would briefly look at each other and then return our gaze to Jane.

Jane took her last breath at 1:47 a.m. on April 3, 2017. She went peacefully. She was surrounded by her father and me, with her mother and brother in the next room.

Numb does not begin to explain the feeling. It was more like holding my breath under seawater, with my eyes open. I struggled to breathe and yet every time I broke the surface, I got pulled right back down. Up and down. Up and down. The wave of crying, tight chest, and short breaths never seemed to end as I bobbed up and down in the swirling sea of grief.

In the moment she left us, her dad and I hugged and cried. Jane was gone, and no words could express our sorrow, so we didn't speak. He had lost his daughter. I had lost my wife.

After a few minutes, when we were able to breathe again, he told me to wake the others so we could begin the Chinese tradition of helping the departed leave this world and enter the next.

When I woke up Emily and Eric, they quickly joined Tim in the bedroom and started chanting the same thing. During this tradition, you're not supposed to cry or show emotion as you encourage the departed to go to the light. I could only last about a minute before I had to retreat to the living room to compose myself. Whatever we were doing typically lasted anywhere from six to eight hours. During that time, I struggled to figure out what to do with myself in between going into the room. Sleep was out of the question, since even though I felt like sleeping, the odd emotional wave of adrenaline, the knot in my stomach, and the lump in my throat prevented me from relaxing enough to attempt sleep. The typical cadence would be in the room for one minute and out of the room for five to ten minutes. We did this till I called 911 around 8 a.m.

Jane passed away outside of hospice care, so we had to call 911 and have the paramedics come and declare that she had died. That was around 9 a.m. That was followed by a visit from the coroner, who declared her deceased at around 11 a.m. The funeral home attendants then took her away to be cremated at around 1 p.m.

The funeral home workers were cordial and professional, but the image of Jane, the love of my life, wrapped in a burgundy body bag being rolled into a white minivan on a ratty old gurney would be forever burned in my brain.

The rage and grief I felt was so intense that as soon as her body was gone, I had to scream into the pillow where she had last rested her head. I needed to smell her one more time. I started to shake and could not stop crying. I wanted to sleep but not in the apartment. It felt awkward, like when I went over to a sorta friend's house and they offered me their "guest room," which was a sofa bed in the living room. I was thankful but felt like I was invading someone's space.

My only respite from the sheer awfulness of it all was when I told myself Jane was no longer in pain—her pain was all over.

The bravery, love, and compassion that Jane showed all of us truly amazed me. She was sad and worried about what it would feel like to die in those last few weeks, but she also worried about how those of us left behind would carry on.

When I came out of the fog of tears and fury, I remembered the honest and loving conversation we'd had. She'd given me the gift of telling me she wanted me to be happy after she was gone.

If I know anything about what love is, it's because of Jane.

From: Jarie Bolander
Date: April 4, 2017
Subject: If I know what love is, it is because of you
To: janes-care-circle ▼

Yesterday, Jane passed away peacefully at our apartment. She was surrounded by the love of family till the end. She was thirty-six years old.

She fought hard against leukemia and tried everything she could to get cured. In the end, leukemia took her body but not her spirit.

We are all heartbroken and numb but are happy that we were with her till the end and that she is no longer in pain.

We are planning a memorial in the next few weeks to honor her life. We will send along the details once they are finalized.

Thanks to all of you for your love and support. Our family, and especially Jane, appreciated it so much. It meant so much to her that all of you helped her on this journey.

Much love,
Team Jane

CHAPTER 27

In the Surf

The next morning, I woke up in Jane's childhood bedroom not knowing where I was. Confused and groggy from too many hits from the vape pen, I reached over to the right side of the bed to hug Jane, but she wasn't there. The nightmare was real. Jane was gone.

I checked my phone and quickly realized that Ria, Jane's friend from high school, would be over soon. It had already been twenty-four hours since Jane passed away.

Ria carried that sense of duty to be the best friend she could be—to us and to any of her friends. Maybe it was her upbringing as a first-generation Indian American or some other magical nature versus nurture thing. Regardless, I was just glad she was there, and that Jane had a friend like her. That was reinforced even more that morning.

"Um. I don't know what to say," Ria said as she hugged the family. "Jane and I met up a couple of weeks ago," she told us. Her hands were shaking. "She gave me these cards for you. She wanted you to have these if things went bad." Each of us—Tim, Emily, Eric, and I—took a card.

We could not contain our tears or look each other in the eye. I excused myself to Jane's room and opened my card:

Dear My Love, aka Babesteins,

You are my heart . . . My dream come true. When I was a little girl, I always dreamed of finding the love of my life. The day I met you at Alice, I had no idea what lay in store for us. What I did know was that you are a kind soul . . . with sweetness, generosity, beauty, and all the other wonderful things a girl could want.

Thank you for loving me with all your heart and taking care of me the way you did. I will miss you every day and am with you always.

Love,

Babesteins

A familiar lump shot into my throat and made me gasp. My chest and throat constricted as if a python were crushing me. Tears streamed down my face as I read the words over and over again—Jane's last words to me.

I could not believe she was gone.

Grief and anger swept over me again—another crashing wave, drowning me and stinging my eyes as I gasped for breath.

The python coiled tighter.

I kept crying, thinking that somehow I could get all the pain out and make it all stop, but the waves kept coming. Wave after wave of sorrow and fury. It was hard to breathe. My nose was full of snot that kept dripping onto a wad of tissue in my hand.

Greenie sat on the chair Jane had been sitting in a few weeks before when she'd posed for a picture snuggling up with him and smiling. He was silent and calm, just like he'd been every day since she introduced him to me as our fuzzy green son.

"Now what do I do?" I asked him between sobs. He wouldn't answer.

After about thirty minutes alone, I emerged to find Tim, Emily, Eric, and Ria at the kitchen table, where we convened to sort out what to do next.

"Thanks for coming over, Ria. I know it's hard to have to deliver these." I gave her a big hug. I'm glad Jane had friends like Ria to help us sort all this out. The burden to hold on to those cards and have that last conversation with Jane must have been intense. Few friends would take that on. "Now I guess we need to figure out what to do. Jane didn't want a funeral or anything like that. More like a party—a 'celebration of life' is how she put it."

I had finally regained my composure and was in "let's get it done" mode, which helped me to numb the pain.

For the next hour, we came up with a plan to find a venue, get a caterer, and remove much of Jane's stuff from our apartment. That last one, removing Jane's stuff, was something that Tim, Emily, Eric, and Ria helped me with. I'm not exactly sure what the urgency of it all was, but it somehow felt right—and both awkward and satisfying at the same time—that Jane's family and friend were helping Jane unclutter her life here so she could move on to the next. It was surreal. Sometimes I felt as if I were walking with the weight of a hundred feet of water pressing all around me. At other times, the dullness felt like diving into the ocean, forgetting to close my eyes, and getting a gallon of water up my nose. Hazy. Dull. Stuffed up. Always on the verge of a sneeze—except with grief, the sneeze turned to tears. The world was murky, mute, and sour. Sometimes the air around me stung like a dozen jellyfish. A gray haze hung over the whole world.

I was sad, mad, and clueless all at the same time.

I was hopeless and Janeless.

Throughout the next three days after Ria's visit, I would go back to Jane's childhood room every hour or so to reread her note, stare at her things, and talk to Greenie.

"What to do? What to do?" I muttered to Greenie as he stared back at me. "She always knew what to do. I'm lost." Greenie still did not answer.

FOR THE REST OF APRIL, STAYING AT OUR apartment was a minefield of memories waiting for me to click a pressure sensor or trip wire. Jane was everywhere—and that felt comforting and devastating at the same time. Even though we had cleaned most of her things out within a few days, I kept finding the odd hair band, greeting card, or hair product squirreled away in some random corner. I even found a couple of broken eyeglasses, which set off a sea of tears again.

Normal things had an odd sort of electric charge to them. I slept on the couch for the first few weeks and threw out our bed and bedding. It felt weird to be wrapped in the same covers we'd shared. That meant I had to buy a new bed, which turned into one of those odd "firsts" after your spouse dies.

"Hey, Jarie. I thought that was you," said Jim, an acquaintance I did extreme sports with, as he got up from a table outside of the Peet's coffee shop on Locust in downtown Walnut Creek. I had just come back from buying my new bed at Mattress Firm a couple of blocks away.

"Oh, hey, Jim." I was shocked to see him. Jim lived in the area, but we didn't hang out that much. We saw each other at parties sometimes, but we weren't close.

"How've you been?" He was smiling. He and the guy he was with both looked up at me, waiting for a response.

"Um . . ." I was shaky, holding back tears that I knew were welling up inside me. "You heard, right? About Jane?"

"Um. Yeah. I heard. Sorry for your loss," he said as his smile faded into a half-frown, half-smile that I was becoming more and more familiar with.

"Yeah. Been tough. You know. Trying to take it a day—" My

voice cracked, and I lowered my head to hide the tears that were starting. "—at a time," I mumbled. This was the first time I had run into anyone in public who knew what had happened. I had gotten plenty of phone calls and texts, but this was a difficult first.

"Yeah. Tough break, for sure. If you need anything, just let me know," Jim said as I raised my head and wiped my tears.

"Thanks. Um. I need to get going. Got to get back to SF," I replied as Jim rose to shake my hand.

"Stay strong, brother," he said as I walked away with my head lowered.

"Will do."

There would be many more conversations like that. The length would vary, but all would be awkward and emotionally charged. I tried to stick to a comfortable routine that allowed me to avoid people and the awkwardness of these kinds of casual meetings.

My routine in that month after Jane's death consisted of waking up early to work out, working from home, eating out, having a couple of drinks to wind down, vaping pot, and then sleeping. Rinse and repeat during the week. Go to Walnut Creek on the weekends. I would sometimes go out with friends, but that was usually way too taxing or sad. Most friends were kind and considerate. They had known Jane, and I could tell it was hard for them to talk about her as well.

Amid all the chaos, I found comfort in my therapy sessions with Scott. He was the therapist who had helped me so much during my divorce from Margaret. Those sessions were the only time I could talk about all the grief, sorrow, conflict, anger, and numbness that filled my days. I always felt better after our sessions, and they helped me reflect on how to handle the challenges ahead. There was something special about a professional who was there to help me and only me. There were some things I could only tell a therapist, and it was comforting to know that whatever weird, crazy thoughts were in my head,

I wouldn't be judged. Friends and family couldn't provide that, since they were too close to me and the situations I talked about.

Those few hours were still not enough to fill the void Jane left, of course.

Day after day, night after night, the only relief came at 5 p.m., when I would stop working, pour myself a healthy glass of wine or Scotch, and figure out how to spend my night.

Most of the time, the couple of drinks turned into a few more until I passed out on the couch watching a Netflix comedy special or the odd documentary about mega structures or the history of World War II, Vietnam, or the Navy SEALs. If I woke up in a panic, which was often, I'd vape some CBD to take the edge off and fall back asleep.

On the odd night when I went out alone, it was to eat and have a few more drinks at the local restaurants around my apartment. I avoided bars. I rationalized my drinking at that point: If I could also eat, then it was not like I went out only to drink. Besides, most of the restaurants I went to had only beer and wine. No hard stuff—easier to stay in control. Who doesn't have a couple of glasses of wine with dinner? For that matter, who doesn't drink to numb the sadness and pain of your wife dying right in front of you? How else are you supposed to push down the anger?

Grief can't be cleared away with a Ready Tab of booze or pot, but I tried anyway. My doctor wanted to put me on antidepressants, but I declined. Those scared me more than anything, given the possible side effects of suicidal thoughts and extreme mood swings. That was the last thing I needed. Better to feel it all and numb the unbearable with the stuff I was used to.

Most people I talked to about their own grief found some respite in work. But most couples don't work together. For me, Jane was everywhere in JSY. When I worked, I felt close to her, but also so deeply sad that she was gone. I routinely talked out loud to her for guidance and support.

To put it simply, Jane and I had been "ride or die" throughout our whole relationship, and now that she had died, I had no idea how I was going to ride again.

As the date for the celebration of life got closer, my sleep was more and more erratic. I would wake up in a panic at 3 a.m. with my heart racing and drenched in sweat.

I felt drowsy all the time, and that clouded my mind. It was hard to focus on work for more than an hour at a time. It was even harder to be creative, which my job now depended on.

When Jane was alive, she was always asking how things were going and pushing me to make things happen. It had annoyed me at the time, but now I yearned for her to sit by my side on the couch like she used to, helping me and encouraging me.

There were so many details to take care of after someone passed away. I learned that even though we had a living trust, not all of our assets were in it. That meant I had to hire a lawyer and go through probate after all, even though we'd created the trust to avoid that scenario. Even a simple task, like canceling Jane's medical insurance, turned into a chore. Not because it was complicated, but because I had to talk to a stranger and say out loud, "*My wife Jane died*, and I need to know what I have to do to [insert task here]."

These interactions were exhausting. I would relive the moment Jane died every time I said those four words. I could feel my throat clench and my body tense up. Afterward, I always watched the clock, waiting for 5 p.m. when I could again pour myself a drink and make the pain go away. I sometimes got to the point where it only had to be 5 p.m. somewhere in order to start the self-medication, especially on the weekends.

I felt like I was walking on the bottom of the ocean, my eyes stinging from the salt water, gasping for air as I struggled to break the surface. Once I broke the surface to take a breath, either a wave of sorrow or the undertow of grief would engulf me, and I'd slowly sink down to the sandy bottom. Each step was a struggle. The world was a tear-soaked blur of baby steps for even basic functions like eating and showering. Would this ever end?

"JANE WOULD HAVE LOVED THIS VENUE. So open and filled with light." Emily was talking to the event coordinator for the Lafayette Veterans Memorial Center, the third place we had toured in one day. I wandered around, stared at the ceiling, and tried to wrap my head around why we were there. *Stay focused,* I told myself as I repeated Jane's advice about events: "Get the venue, then get the food and drinks."

"Yeah. She would have liked it," I agreed, walking outside to cry.

"Why did you have to die?" I said aloud. "I don't know what to do." It was hard to be in the moment. The usual dull haze descended on me again.

I took a lap around the parking lot and then went back inside.

"Sorry about that," I said as I walked back inside, wiping my nose. "We'll take it."

Remember what Jane taught you, I kept telling myself. *This is just like any other event we've done. Make a checklist and get it done. Focus on throwing the best celebration of life you can. Don't get caught up in your own private pity party. Make Jane proud. You have a job to do. Results!*

With the venue secured, it was on to the food. Jane had volunteered at a local food nonprofit called La Cocina. That's where she'd met Pinky Cooper of Pinx Catering. Pinky had done our rehearsal dinner and our wedding. Her pop-up in Oakland was where I'd first met Jane's parents. I knew that she would take care of us, and it warmed my heart that someone Jane helped would be part of her final event.

The rest of the celebration came together without too much trouble. We'd have about 250 people in all, which was bigger than our wedding. As the days wore on, I was getting a little more comfortable talking about and sorting out the details. Lots of friends and family were helping out, and that made me feel less alone.

I still played the game of making it to 5 p.m. and then giving in to the relief of alcohol. Drinking relaxed all the tension that had built up in my body during the day. I'd sink into the couch and feel the booze warm my body and dull my mind. I'd turn on the TV and surf to some random YouTube channel or Netflix movie I'd never make it through. At times, I'd forget about the grief for a brief moment. Then I'd be reminded when I looked at our wedding photo or one of Jane's many books scattered around the house. I knew I'd have to limit my drinking at some point. But in those first weeks, it felt too good to take a drink and forget about the previous fifteen months. And drinking sometimes helped me remember all the good times Jane and I had too, at fancy restaurants with good Scotch and yummy cocktails.

"I miss you so much, babe!" I'd say louder and louder the more I drank. "Why did you have to die? I'm so lost without you." There was never an answer to my drunken questions. I'd rarely make it to our bedroom and ended up sleeping on the couch more nights than not.

CHAPTER 28

Celebration of Life

J ane's extended family and friends had helped a ton in orga-
nizing the day of remembrance and celebration of Jane's life.
She would have been proud of it all, from the decorations and
food to the music and whiskey.

"Today will be a rough day. Everyone is going to be looking
at us. They'll follow our lead," I said to Tim, Emily, and Eric.
The four of us were around Tim and Emily's kitchen table, going
over the final details. "People won't know what to say or do. It's
going to be awkward and sad. It's up to us to set the mood." I
knew I sounded like a coach whose team was about to hit the
field, and in a way, that's what we were. We were still Team Jane.

I had hired Anders, a Lutheran pastor, to preside because
he had the right mix of religion and spirituality to make the
more religious side of the family comfortable but was not so
over the top that we'd be praying every five minutes. Anders
would provide the introduction. Phil, Jane's childhood friend
and senior prom date, would perform a song. Which song, he
had kept as a surprise from me. I'd do the eulogy. Eric would
remember his sister, Tim would do a slideshow, and then Ria,
Mary, and Natalie would say a few words.

I had spent the better part of a week preparing Jane's eulogy with my friend Danny, who made sure it had the right amount of levity. I had known Danny since we shared a cubicle at Cypress Semiconductor, and he had read a poem at our wedding.

I was determined not to fuck up the eulogy by breaking down or not being able to continue. I told myself to stay focused, even while Phil was playing "Mario Kart Love Song," which was the "surprise" song. Jane would have howled at that.

"Set the example," I muttered, psyching myself up. "Do everything you can to celebrate her life. She would do the same for you. This is it. The end of the ride. Get up there and speak from your heart."

As Phil finished, my hands started to tremble. I had that familiar lump in my throat. I tried to smile as Anders introduced me.

More than 250 people who loved Jane were watching me as I glanced at the table where her urn had been placed. I looked up at the blur of faces, then down to my notes. My first words were a little shaky as I gave in to the inevitable tears. I was glad I had taken Danny's advice to start with a story that was perfectly Jane. I told it in the present tense for effect, and it felt as if I were just relaying a story about her at an event. I could even imagine her there, listening in, laughing along.

In a mushroom cloud of vegan cocoa power, Jane can't stop laughing. She is attempting to make vegan brownies and is failing at it. Miserably, I might add. This catastrophic cloud of cocoa powder was a result of Jane's frustration with trying to open the heat-sealed bag. Something she was never good at.

In between bouts of laughter and my cleaning up the cocoa, she sings one of her made-up songs and dances her little Jane jig, as if no one is watching.

I paused to catch my breath. I'd forgotten to breathe, I was so lost in the moment of it all, so overcome with mixed emotions of grief and gratitude. All I wanted to do was get through this as fast as I could, but Danny told me to pause, take a breath, don't rush. I had scribbled those words on each page of the eulogy with a black Sharpie, along with *Look Up!*

Well, I'm watching, and it's one of the most beautiful and classically Jane moments of the many moments we spent in our short time together.

On behalf of Jane's family, thank you all for coming to celebrate Jane's life.

Pause. Breath. *Hold back the tears. Shit. Push down the failure lump. Stick to the plan. You practiced this a dozen or more times. Just read.*

Jane enjoyed every day. She felt joy on so many levels. Nothing gave her more joy than checking things off "the list," which she kept on random scraps of paper and draft emails. She had list after list of tasks to check off. She was the only human I know that used a draft email as a task list. Each completed task was a small victory in her quest to make things happen.

I have never heard such a laugh as hers. It filled the room. It made you instantly smile even if the joke was on you, which, in my case, it often was.

The crowd laughed. *Good*, I thought. *That's where I wanted them to laugh. Keep going.* Deep breath. *Almost done. Good work. Remember, Look up and scan the room.*

She loved the odd word or phrase. These words were the ones that made her laugh the most:

Random "steins" after many words. For example, my nickname was Babesteins. Where did she come up with this stuff?

If she judged that I was doing something stupid, she would immediately call me "old balls."

That would lead to her telling me to "Stop doing stupid things because I don't want to change your diaper."

Or my personal favorite: "There is no trying, only results!" Good times!

People laughed, and I imagined Emily cringing at the "old balls" joke, but I didn't care. Breath. Pause. *Keep going. Home stretch.*

Love is a strange and wonderful thing.
In order to receive love, one must be open to it.
Jane was always open to love and to being loved.
Jane loved her friends and family without question or condition.
She was always there.
No matter the day.
No matter the time.
No matter the time zone.

She wrote and published this book while she was in the hospital this past January. She gave it to me for my birthday in February. It's classic Jane. It's a bit silly, a bit mushy, and all heart.

I held up the book so everyone could see the blue cover with stick figures that looked like Jane and me, holding hands and smiling. She'd even put a beard on my stick figure face.

How many people do you know who would ignore their suffering and create such a beautiful gift?

We should all take solace in the fact that she achieved the things that matter the most in life: being kind, caring about others, loving and being loved, and making a difference. Most leave this world never having done those things.

She did them all.

I hope Jane's life inspires you to live your life with laughter, kindness, and love.

As for the vegan brownies, they tasted great but looked like a hot mess. Kinda like Jane sometimes.

The crowd laughed at that as well, which was the plan I had practiced with Danny: Make sure to pay off the setup in the beginning. Kinda like a joke setup, followed by a punch line. Set up the story, then deliver the payoff. It worked and made it easier for me to get through it knowing that when the crowd laughed or giggled, I could take a pause and smile as well.

Rest easy, my love. You brought out the best in me.
You gave me the greatest honor to be your husband.
You will always be in my heart.

I couldn't hold it together anymore. Full-on voice crack and tears came with that final line. It felt so final and real, like after I said ,"You will always be in my heart," she would really be dead—never to return.

When she gave me the book, I couldn't have imagined I would be sharing it during her eulogy, but it felt like the right thing to do to share her thoughts and her own words, even if it was about me. Maybe she wanted to make sure I knew all those things, which I did. Maybe she wanted to ensure I wouldn't forget her, which I couldn't. No worries about that, Jane. You are forever burned into my mind and my heart.

After a tearful speech by Jane's brother, Eric, a heartwarming presentation by Tim, and some parting words from her friends Mary, Ria, and Natalie, we gathered in a line to greet the guests. That was a receiving line no one really wanted to line up for—a moment to offer awkward condolences to a grieving family on the loss of their wife/daughter/sister so young.

As we lined up, someone handed me a tumbler half-filled with Scotch. It dulled the emotions enough for me to relax, and I discovered that underneath my grief, I felt comfort. It was beautiful to hear the stories of Jane's impact on people's lives. I was glad we had a chance to thank people personally for their help and kindness.

There was a lot of love in the room, and a lot of Jane.

CHAPTER 29

The Gift

"So now what?" I said to Greenie as I placed Jane's urn on her dresser and removed my tie to get more comfortable. "I guess it's just you and me now, kid."

I walked in the door to Tim and Emily's house around 5 p.m., said a quick hello, and went straight into Jane's room to change. It had been an emotional day. The biggest day in my life with Jane, other than our wedding day, was officially over. What was I going to do with the rest of my life?

"I'm glad you were there to comfort her when I wasn't," I told Greenie. I picked him up and noticed the worn spot on the back of his head where Jane had cuddled him and rubbed him against her face.

"It's been a shitty year, huh?" I stroked Greenie's head and looked into his eyes. I could see why Jane found comfort in the way he just sat there, not talking, always smiling back at you with his crooked smile. He was always waiting to be of service, ready to help. And he was the only son Jane and I would ever have.

I had stayed in Jane's childhood room with her many times, and I had spent every weekend the month after she died there too, surrounded by memories from when she was young. All her awards, books, pictures from the prom, and even some of her clothes were still in the room. I felt numb and lost when I looked at the possessions that had meant so much to her, just like I did when I touched her things in our apartment.

My celebration of life suit hung in the closet below her wedding dress and high school graduation gown, which were both wrapped in tissue paper and packed neatly in clear Rubbermaid boxes.

"She looked so beautiful in this dress, Greenie. You should have seen her." I tilted open the box that held her wedding dress to take a look. The lace was still shiny and delicate. "My niece said she looked like a princess."

The thought of our wedding day was suddenly too much. I started to sob.

When the tears stopped, I realized I was still clutching Greenie tightly.

"I know it might not seem that way now, but I've been lucky," I told him. "Even though Jane was sick and sometimes a pain in the ass, we had fun. She looked out for us both. Always wanted to make sure we were okay."

I couldn't stop myself from chuckling for a second, imagining Greenie flopped at the end of Jane's hospital bed. "All the nurses wanted to take care of her. Remember how she would talk to them and play music? It was like a *party* in her room."

Greenie and I sat in Jane's chair for a little while. I framed the picture of her sitting in this exact chair, smiling and holding her friend Greenie. She looked so happy. That was a month before she died.

"I'll tell you one thing, kid." I pulled Greenie up to my face, looking him in his button eyes, choking back another wave of tears. "I'm glad I went to that stupid breakfast. She was so brave. I hope I'm half as brave when my time comes. What a gift she was. She showed up during the good times and the bad." I whispered in Greenie's ear, "Such a void. Such a gaping hole. Ride or die. I guess it's my turn to ride on."

I knew he would understand because he'd been there until the end.

I placed him next to the urn on Jane's dresser, in her childhood room, facing the empty bed. For now, the urn of Jane's ashes would stay here until I could figure out a way to carry out Jane's wishes for them, which were twofold. The first wish was to mix some into gourmet ice cream. What to do with said ice cream after said mixing was vague. I'd figure it out when I got there, but I loved that she wanted her ashes to be forever mixed with her favorite dessert.

The second one was to spread some ashes whenever we traveled, including her favorite places like Taiwan, France, Iceland, New Orleans, various parts of San Francisco, and anywhere we thought she would like, preferably with a nice view. The funeral home had advised me never to travel with a full urn of ashes since it would get me a bullet train to the TSA strip search lounge. I never asked why and frankly wanted to travel lighter than the ten or so pounds of ash and urn anyway. The solution turned out to be some portable urns that looked like cigar holders. I bought three gold-colored ones which were engraved with "Jane Yin Bolander, March 2, 1981–April 3, 2017." Hardly subtle, but functional.

At the door, I paused to take it all in. Her room was a time capsule. Pretty much as she'd left it when she first moved out. I turned off the light and gently closed the door.

Epilogue

It took me 408 days, two meltdowns, weekly therapy, being diagnosed with sleep apnea, countless blurry mornings, and almost losing my now-fiancée, Minerva, to realize that drinking was not helping me deal with my grief and sorrow. So I stopped. Cold turkey.

As I write this on February 14, 2023, that was 1,736 days ago without a drink.

I don't think I'll ever drink again. It's not good for me—even as much as I loved the taste of a cold, malty Belgian ale after a hard run or long day of work. The first sip was the best. The explosion of malt hops and the tickling foam bubbles relaxed me instantly. Tension and stress evaporated in the surge of warmth that radiated through my core. Pure joy.

What keeps me from taking another sip is the commitment I made to myself to be good, do good, and be happy. That was also part of my commitment to ride or die with Jane. She fulfilled her commitment, and now I need to fulfill mine. The rub is that I'm still here in the world dealing with the aftermath of trauma, loss, and grief, as well as the new love and joy that life has to offer. My commitment takes more effort and diligence. It's hard enough some days to remember to see the goodness in the world. If I let something like alcohol reduce that ability, then I'm cheating those who love me and myself.

I'm lucky. I have people who care about me and want me to live a happy life. They accept and love me for me—not what I do or achieve. The power of that acceptance is magical, and I'm thankful for it every single day.

It's not that I don't want to be happy, but there are days when the grief demons come, wanting me to come back to our private pity party. I have to remind myself that happiness starts with loving myself first. Without that, I can't commit to loving others.

I wrote this book for everyone who has experienced the challenges of sickness, the testing of commitment, the stress of the unknown, and the grief over loss, but especially for men like me who want to solve problems by taking action. We want to right all the wrongs and save everyone in the name of love. The trap we fall into is that we may try to become the manifestation of the person we lost. At first, I was tempted to become "the new Jane," which gave me never-ending inner conflict and anxiety.

It's easy to lose yourself in someone else's sickness and hard to find yourself again.

People try to help, but that help is difficult to handle too. For a long time after Jane died, I had plenty of people to do things with, but no one to do *nothing* with. And I'd spent so much time being a caregiver and friend that I'd lost myself as a man and husband. I gave everything to helping Jane through her illness, and many men and women do the same for their spouses and partners. In the end, there was no cure. Am I a failure then? How do I live with that guilt?

I want Jane to be remembered, but how do I also remember who I am? How do I honor my "ride or die" commitment to her to be happy if I've lost myself?

I did it. I kept my vow. I know that many of you reading this book have the same questions, so here is my answer:

You'll never be happy if you're trying to live your departed loved one's life. *Your life is yours, and you have to live it.* Her life was her life and it's done.

I think that's the hardest thing to come to grips with.

You and I can only achieve the happiness we need and deserve—the happiness our loved ones want us to have—if we know who we are, what we want, and how we want to live. That's how we honor their memory.

The greatest honor I can give Jane is to lead a long, happy life, filled with love, compassion, and service. All those things have to be part of my life, or I'll end up just trying to recapture what I lost, and my existence will be gray and empty. I'll never reach my full potential, and Jane would not want that.

Since Jane died, I've thought a lot about what a ride or die commitment means. I've also thought a lot about marriage and the vows *in sickness and in health . . . till death do us part.*

I think it's about being present and supportive for the journey together—through every high and low—and then continuing the journey, through grief and anger, to find joy and love again. It's about living the life your beloved wanted for you, you wanted for them, and the one you should want for you even among the random and chaotic world we live in.

That's the commitment I keep to Jane every day and one that will never end. It's the part of taking those vows no one tells you about, that you're never apart, even after death.

Acknowledgments

To Minerva, who has been an inspiration and such a warm and loving person throughout my time writing this book and in my grieving process. I know it's not easy to support someone who is writing a book about their departed partner. I love you dearly and can't wait to see what the future holds for us.

I am eternally grateful to Leslie Watts, who helped make sense of my ramblings, and to Shawn Coyne for creating the Story Grid and giving me excellent feedback on the manuscript. It's always tough to share your story and art. I'm glad I found you both.

Special thanks to Victoria Wang for reading early drafts of the manuscript and correcting my horrible grammar and spelling.

Additional thanks to Shelley Sperry, who helped tremendously with several drafts of the manuscript and helped me understand pace and character voice.

To my memoir coach, Brooke Warner, who helped me refine and polish Jane's and my story to a fine sheen. It's a joy to work with you.

To our families, who stood by us throughout Jane's sickness and the aftermath. I am grateful for your love and caring.

To my Sheepdog workout crew. You guys have helped me more than I can ever say or repay.

To Jane's Care Circle, who made our journey through the most difficult times more tolerable. I may never get to thank each of you in person, but there is not a day that goes by that I don't think about the warmth and love you showed us.

And finally, to Jane, who even in the face of her own passing was loving, caring, and brave. She gave me the gift of boundless love. I endeavor to earn it every day.

Rest easy, my love. You are always in my heart.

About the Author

JARIE BOLANDER caught the startup bug right after graduating from San Jose State University in 1995 with a degree in electrical engineering. With 6 startups, 7.75 books, and 10 patents under his belt, his experience runs the gamut from semiconductors to life sciences to nonprofits. He also hosts a podcast called The Entrepreneur Ethos, which is based on his last book by the same name. When he's not helping clients convert a concept to a viable strategy, he can be found on the Jiu-Jitsu mat (he's a blue belt), interviewing entrepreneurs on his podcast, or researching the latest in earthship construction techniques. He's engaged to a wonderful woman named Minerva, her daughter, and their Bernedoodle, Sage. Currently, Jarie lives and works in San Francisco, where he works as head of market strategy for Decision Counsel, a B2B growth consulting firm.

Author photo © Sammy Hernandez

SELECTED TITLES FROM SPARKPRESS

SparkPress is an independent boutique publisher delivering high-quality, entertaining, and engaging content that enhances readers' lives, with a special focus on female-driven work. www.gosparkpress.com

Even if Your Heart Would Listen: Losing My Daughter to Heroin, Elise Schiller. $16.95, 978-1-68463-008-0. In January of 2014, Elise Schiller's daughter, Giana Natali, died of a heroin overdose. *Even if Your Heart Would Listen* is a memoir about Giana's illness and death and its impact on her family—especially her mother—as well as a close examination and critique of the treatment she received from health care practitioners while she was struggling to get well.

Love You Like the Sky: Surviving the Suicide of a Beloved, Sarah Neustadter. $16.95, 978-1-943006-88-5. Part memoir and part self-help in nature, this compilation of emails—written by a young psychologist to her beloved following his suicide—chronicles the process of surviving and grieving the tragic death of a loved one, and of using grief for deeper psycho-spiritual healing and transformation.

What They Didn't Burn: Uncovering My Father's Holocaust Secrets, Mel Laytner, $16.95, 978-1-68463-103-2. What if you uncovered a cache of buried Nazi documents that revealed your father as a man very different than the one you knew—or thought you knew? In this poignant memoir, Mel Laytner, a former reporter, peels away layers of his father's stories to expose painful truths about surviving the Holocaust and its aftermath.

Roots and Wings: Ten Lessons of Motherhood that Helped Me Create and Run a Company, Margery Kraus with Phyllis Piano. $16.95, 978-1-68463-024-0. Margery Kraus, a trailblazing corporate and public affairs professional who became a mother at twenty-one, shares ten lessons from motherhood and leadership that enabled her to create, run, and grow a global company. Her inspiring story of crashing through barriers as she took on increasingly challenging opportunities will have women of all ages cheering.

A Story That Matters: A Gratifying Approach to Writing About Your Life, Gina Carroll. $16.95, 9-781-943006-12-0. With each chapter focusing on stories from the seminal periods of a lifetime—motherhood, childhood, relationships, work, and spirit—*A Story That Matters* provides the tools and motivation to craft and complete the stories of your life.

Social Media Isn't Social: Rediscovering the lost art of face-to-face communication, Al Maag. $15, 978-1940716459. With humor and insight born of decades of experience, Al Maag shares what he learned during his Chicago childhood in the 1950s and 60s, a stark contrast to the current C-generation that has grown up with electronic gadgets. *Social Media Isn't Social* shows why online social media cannot replace face-to-face human connection, and reveals the critical real-life social skills you need to succeed today in business and in life.